To Debbie,
Moms are extraordinary! Thanks for all you do.
Happy Mother's Day,
The Moms

JUST ORDINARY MOMS

True Stories by Moms for Moms

Robin Cournoyer, Caren Garvan,
Lael Jacobs, Jeanne Lebens,
Bonnie Quinlan, Celia Rose,
Linda Spevacek, Maureen Wolf

First Edition, May 2013.

Ingram Publishing Services Inc.
Printed in the United States of America.

ISBN: 1484035623

ISBN-13: 978-1484035627

Author photo by Steve Quinlan
Message in a bottle photo by Robin Cournoyer
Handwritten note photo by Tony Cournoyer

Cover design by Dzenita Hajric

DEDICATION

We dedicate this book to our own moms, dads, husbands and children, and to all mothers everywhere.

ACKNOWLEDGEMENTS

Without our children, this book would not exist. We love you more than anything else in the world.

To our family and friends, we are grateful for your unending support and genuine encouragement. Your good-natured patience allowed us the free rein to bring our stories to life.

Professionally, we would like to thank Lisa, our hilarious author friend who helped guide us, Debbie, our masterful connector and advisor, and Libbye and David, our amazing editors. In addition, to the book clubs and reading groups whose enthusiastic responses exceeded our hopes and dreams, we appreciate all of you. To the unknown mom whose story touched our hearts so deeply, your loving letter was also a message to us that we had to complete this book.

Finally, we celebrate each other, the eight "just ordinary" moms, who listened, laughed, cried and helped shape even the roughest of stories we bravely shared with each other. This book embodies the beautiful story mosaic that is our forever friendship.

CONTENTS

INTRODUCTION

We share these stories with you in the hope that you just might find yourself somewhere inside these pages and discover the joy of knowing that mothers everywhere have a connection that, even if unspoken, exists on a collective level. Call it a "sisterhood of motherhood."

Our experience of sharing these stories—first with each other, then with book clubs, and now with the world, has been a delight. It is addicting, this feeling of connection, of not being the only one trying to make your way through the real-life journey called motherhood, which none of us is ever truly prepared for.

We also hope to pave the way for you to begin to feel comfortable sharing your own truths about your experiences. As you read the stories in this book, we invite you to be mindful of memories that pop into your head—of your own child rearing days or perhaps from your own childhood. Could any of those tales be useful to someone you know? By sharing yourself, you may be able to help others realize that they are not alone.

Helping others is a core element of this book, as well as additional projects we hope to create. Thank you for helping us aim high as we strive to raise generous amounts for deserving charities.

All of the stories in this book are true, although names, locations, and sometimes genders and certain other details have been changed to protect the privacy of everyone involved.

We also feel compelled to warn you that these stories are drawn from real life, and therefore contain raw, indelicate language and experiences that you may find shocking, heart wrenching, or otherwise difficult to handle. Sometimes motherhood can be like that!

Mostly, after reading these stories, we hope you will feel like you have made some new friends who have laughed and cried with you as you made your own way. Whatever *your* story, you need never feel alone again.

Sincerely yours,

P.S. Do you have a story to tell? We want to hear from you! Check out the Bonus section "My Story" Workshop where we show you how to get started.

*"Don't follow in my footsteps,
make your own."*

THE BEACH CHAIR

I am deeply nestled into my time-worn, sturdy and indestructible, faded navy blue Coleman canvas chair, thinking about how it has held me, without complaint, for more than twenty years, through forty-pound weight swings and spilled morning coffee and evening wine.

The netted cup holders on each arm have tended so many treasures through the years. One cup holder secured a beverage, and the other was entrusted with an ever-changing parade of items: scallop shells and periwinkles, opaque white and irregularly shaped sea glass, salty-tasting pacifiers rinsed clean of sand, baggies full of goldfish crackers and pistachio nuts, Lego people and plastic boats, and, in my smoking years, the ever-present pack of Marlboro Lights 100's and a lighter.

When my own kids, my nieces and nephews, and now my

cousins' children, have jumped on my lap, my chair simply squared its legs and dug deeper into the sand to hold us. When a sleepy baby needed a safe napping spot, my chair became a cozy nest, safely cradling the newest family member, peacefully sleeping, lulled by the hypnotizing rhythm of the waves coming into shore.

I am comfortably settled in the chair, shaded by the canopy above. I glance at the delicately webbed rust that has started to form around the metal rivets that hold the chair legs together. My eyes are drawn to my perennially painted red toes, peeking out from the heavy, gray mound of sand in which my nephew has encased them.

Once upon a time, this little island in the Outer Banks of North Carolina had stereotypically sugary white sand beaches stretching in an unspoiled vista as far as the eyes could see, blinding us as the sun hit the diamond-like quartz embedded within. The protected sand dunes crowned with their willowy sea oats gently swaying in the breeze are the only reminders of how soft and white the sand once was.

Years of storms and beach erosion have led to projects involving dredging the ocean floor and blowing the sand back onto the beach using loud, crane-like machines that look like giant metal dinosaurs. These machines belch up the deepest, darkest ocean floor sand, releasing hidden treasures for lucky beachcombers to find, like prehistoric Megalodon shark teeth, halves of impossibly large sand dollars from a bygone era, and crusty, ancient, barnacled clam shells.

I hear laughter and turn to see gleeful children tossing a football at the water's edge. They aren't really children anymore, and my heart sighs with a gentle thud at that realization. I have two sons in their twenties—one in college and the other who has graduated and begun his career—and a daughter poised right on the edge of adulthood. She retains a youthful innocence, while chomping at the bit to start college in the fall. The bonus baby, as light-eyed and light-haired as the older three are dark, with soft, honey peach fuzz on his face glistening in the sun, is just another reminder that these four unique souls continue to be the best gifts I have ever been given.

I watch with a melancholy smile as they decide, as usual and for whatever reason, to go after the youngest as they run around like lunatics, knee deep in the surf, laughing and screaming until they catch him and throw him into the crashing waves. And, like a flock of birds with some secret signal known only to them, they dive into an oncoming wave emerging from the other side, each taking both hands to push back their hair and then swimming toward the youngest. They bob up and down in the bottle-green water, sometimes jumping or diving, depending on the wave height, all the while chatting like friends who have not seen each other in a long time. My heart swells at their friendship and the love they have for each other.

I notice my husband in his matching, equally old, trusty chair looking out toward them and, in our own unspoken way, we reach our hands out to each other, lace our fingers together, and unite in enjoying the expression of love that we created. I know that as we sit there quietly watching the scene in front of us, in our minds we are both running a triple-feature reel of memories of these exact same moments, repeated year after year.

I think it is our favorite movie of all time.

"I'm going to eat you up with kisses!"

JUST ORDINARY MOMS

THE GOOD MOTHER

*I*n a casual phone conversation with a girlfriend and fellow mom, I hear of an unfortunate mother who recently learned that her eight-year-old child has diabetes. With puzzlement that echoes like a plea, my girlfriend cries, "And she is one of those really *good* moms!" A wave of anxiety ripples through me, intensified in seconds to pure panic. My heart is beating rapidly, my mind racing. It goes something like this: I am not doing enough to ensure that my son eats healthy, whole foods with no sugar. I knew I should have switched to organic food even though it is expensive and difficult to find. I should insist that he get at least an hour of physical activity a day. I let him watch too much TV this week. Why didn't I find a new brand of vitamins when he decided to refuse his current ones? If I am not a good mother, what is *he* liable to come down with? Scabies? Ricketts? Cancer?

My self-awareness is now a tornado of apprehension that picks up speed and strength with each area it touches, leaving a disheartening pile of destruction and despair in its wake. What began as a tickle of worry about my son's nutritional health has now become a complete transformation of my mommy self-image. I begin to worry about my son's grades and whether I am seeking enough opportunities for him to show himself as a leader (because colleges look at that, you know). I worry whether I am coddling him too much by still picking him up at his bus stop, or would he get kidnapped if I didn't? Do I talk with him frequently enough? Teach him about empathy, respect, and kindness? Gosh, we really should go to church. How can I be letting these things slide? What kind of mother am I?

As this infection of anxiety overtakes me, it dawns on me suddenly that nothing quite brings on self-doubt and criticism like the words "a good mom." Nothing else puts such fear and panic in my heart or shakes my self-esteem to the core. When this whirlwind of worry overtakes me, where do I turn to right the world again, to stop the spinning, the doubt, the *guilt*? I used to think that seeking support from other "good moms" would be the answer, but that has turned out to be very complicated.

I remember when my son was three and I was a lucky participant in a mothers' group. While our children played, the mothers discussed everything from breast-feeding to meal planning. At the time, I thought it was great to be with other adults and to have a place to get parenting support and advice. Yet I never quite felt shored up after those meetings. Instead, I felt inadequate and insecure.

Looking back, these meetings were as much a competitive lion's den as they were a safe, supportive haven. Mothers were quick to share what good moms they were in the guise of giving empathic advice: "Maybe you should try a coupon system for Johnny to get him to stay in bed. It worked wonders for Hannah. She hasn't gotten up at night in a year!"

And then there was the unfortunate mother whose child periodically hit other children in the group. The judgments from the other mothers were endless and harsh, albeit cloaked in seeming concern and empathy. "I feel so bad for Amy. Her son, Timmy, is impossible. I don't understand why she doesn't just make him leave the play date or give him a time out. He needs some consequences."

I used to contribute my two cents of advice in these situations without a moment of hesitation. Having an answer or a suggestion seemed to slow my own spinning tornado a bit, lift my confidence a little. I also felt I was being helpful. But something in these interactions felt gossipy, judgmental, and wrong. Although I may have felt a bit less anxious, I didn't necessarily feel safe.

Then one day, I had a revelation. It was so profound that it literally brought tears to my eyes. It also helped me understand this process I seemed stuck in. I realized, with much humility, that I had truly never met a mother who had not tried everything in her power to be a good mom. Amy was not a personal failure, ignorant, lazy, in denial about her son's behavior, or disinterested. She was plain *beat*. She had already tried everything in her arsenal, including time-outs and leaving play dates, asked for advice, and read everything she could find about hitting behavior in children. She may not have found the right solution yet, but she would not give up until she did.

On that day of epiphany, I completely empathized with the tornado of fear and panic my friend must have endured when her son hit other children. I could imagine how alone she must have felt amidst all the well-meaning advice. How sad that no one (including myself) could just say, "I'm sorry. This must be really difficult for you to go through. I know you've tried really hard to solve this."

The sad and humbling truth for me in this revelation was that those words were not forthcoming because all of us other moms were too busy spinning in our own "good mom tornados." It wasn't that we did not want to be empathic or helpful, but seeing Timmy hit other kids put us in a panic about ourselves. Could this happen to me? Am *I* a good mom? (And therefore, a good, worthwhile human being?) When we could come up with a technique or a judgment, it was a way to say, "Yes, see? I know what to do because I am a good mother." Like kids playing a magic trick, we could once again make everything OK by diversion and concealment.

We think we can hold back the wind with solutions, keeping ourselves and our children safe by building a house of "good mothering" around us. But it is like the little pig's house of sticks. While sometimes these solutions help, sometimes they don't. Yet that failure does not define us as mothers or as human beings. It is what it is. We do what we can, and then we have to let it go. We have to embrace our powerlessness and hold ourselves together with empathy and self-love. And that is how I halt this nasty tornado I am in now—at least until the next time someone says, "...and she was a *good* mom."

JUST ORDINARY MOMS

*"How do I know? I have eyes
in the back of my head!"*

JUST ORDINARY MOMS

MENTAL BRAKES

I recognized my own handwriting on the back of the large envelope but could not immediately register where it might have come from. It was a standard manila envelope, the kind that typically contains documents for signing or a photo with cardboard reinforcement to prevent bending.

I looked closer. "Some mail we received for you" were the words I had written across the back flap. I remembered now. It was a collection of routine information and papers I had forwarded on to our nineteen-year-old son, Jack, enrolled in film school in New York City.

I flipped the envelope over. Sure enough, it was addressed in my handwriting to Jack at his high-rise, dormitory-style apartment building on the Upper West Side. Next to the address was a yellow sticker on the envelope that said, in a computerized font spit out from some machine:

Undeliverable to Addressee. Name not found at this address.

What a pain. I must have messed up the mailing address somehow. I would have to resend it. I could not recall what was inside the packet and hoped it was nothing important.

I set the envelope aside and continued through the mail pile—bills, junk mail, bank statements, an envelope from my mom (no doubt containing a clipping from *The Washington Post* that she thought would be of interest), a letter from my own college (no doubt containing a request for donations), more bills, and then another envelope, this one a plain white, regular-sized one, also addressed in my handwriting to Jack at the dorm building in New York, and also stuck with a yellow **"Undeliverable to Addressee"** sticker next to his name.

Why are they sending these back? I had mailed him plenty of things there before. I looked at both envelopes again. Both had his unit number, 1143, scrawled on the front in black magic marker. Clearly these envelopes had been delivered to his building, handled by mailroom personnel, rejected, and marked as undeliverable.

Mental brakes. Is it possible he is not living there anymore?

I inspected the envelopes in even greater detail. When had I sent these? I studied the postmarks. Both were dispatched quite some time ago; one was stamped with a date almost two months before. But we had been in contact a number of times since I had sent these. He had even visited home since I had sent these.

Mental brakes. Despite being in contact, I would not know if he was not actually living in his dorm anymore unless he told me. I don't really know anything about his life in New York, do I? Could he have moved out and decided not to tell?

I ripped the ends off each envelope to see what was inside: a clipping from *The Washington Post* from my mom about an upcoming young movie director, a donation appeal from his prep school, his new insurance card, and an envelope from some organization.

He definitely needed the insurance card for his acne appointments and prescriptions. I would stick it in the mail tomorrow. Then I decided to open the organization's envelope in case it was something time-sensitive or contained information he needed; otherwise, I would not bother to resend it to him.

I unfolded the letter and read "Welcome to Family Pledge, the pregnancy planning and prevention program."

Whaaaaaaaaat? Step hard on the mental brakes. Was someone pregnant? Had someone been pregnant? Was my son, who might not be living in his dorm anymore, involved with someone who was pregnant? Perhaps extremely closely, intimately involved?

My mind, having started down the road of perturbing

possibility, continued on its journey. Was it possible Jack had moved out and was involved in a pregnancy? Was he living somewhere else with a pregnant companion? Had he dropped out of school, too? Parents never get any information from schools anymore.

What were they living on? Had he gotten a job to help pay the rent? Who was this sleazy girl who had gotten my son into this predicament? Who was this magnificent girl who was carrying my grandchild? What would happen to his dreams of a film career if he had to support a family? Was she an actress? What was her name? Were they thinking about an abortion? I should tell them not to get the abortion, that it would be OK; we would help support them and the baby. What would they name the baby? Where was the girl from? Would we get to see them often? I wanted to be a part of their lives and the baby's.

I pictured Jack holding a newborn. He was going to make a wonderful father. I could see the love and delight on his face as he gazed at the baby. Would it be a boy or a girl? It looked like a girl to me—wrapped in a soft white blanket with little pink bears on it.

Life would not be easy for them. Living in New York City was terribly expensive. Then I had an idea. They could live with us! Our lower level would function perfectly as an apartment for a couple and a newborn. It has a bathroom, a small kitchenette, and direct access from the garage. We would probably have to get Jack a car so he could work somewhere. I wondered if the girl had her own car.

I hoped she was taking good care of herself, getting enough sleep and eating properly. I wondered about her family, whether they would be supportive. Had she told her parents yet? When was Jack planning to tell us? Or were they planning to get rid of it? I needed to tell him right now that they did not have to do that. We would help.

I picked up the phone and dialed Jack's cell.

"Hi, Mom." His voice sounded so young, certainly not old enough to be a father. And yet he was.

I swallowed hard and chose my next words extremely carefully.

"Hi, honey, how are ya'? Anything new?"

"Nope. Nothing new."

"Are you..." I hesitated, not sure what to ask. "Are you at home right now?"

"Yeah, I'm home."

"At the dorm?"

"Yeah."

Mental brakes. What to ask next?

"Do you ever get any mail at the dorm?"

"Yeah. I mean, I think so. I haven't checked in a while."

"So you *are* still living in the building?"

Momentary silence. "Yeah. Where else would I be living?"

"Well, that's what I was wondering because I got some

mail that I had sent to you returned with a sticker on it saying 'Undeliverable' and 'No such person at this address,' or something like that, and I thought maybe, for some reason, you had moved out."

"No, Mom. I still live here."

Mental brakes. One bridge crossed, one to go.

"OK. Well, maybe you could contact the mailroom and find out why they aren't delivering your mail to you."

"OK, I will."

Mental brakes. Deep breath. "I opened the returned envelopes to see what I had sent to you, and your new insurance card is in there. I assume you need that for your doctor's appointments and prescription, so I'll send it right away. The other stuff isn't anything you really need."

"OK."

Deep breath. "Except maybe one other thing—there's an envelope about pregnancy planning." Deep breath. "Is that something you need?"

"What?"

"It is something called Family Pledge, about pregnancy planning and prevention. I don't know exactly. Do you want me to read what it says?"

"Oh, I know. That is something I was supposed to sign because of the skin medicine—you know, my Accutane. They want you to take a pledge not to get pregnant, which I can't anyway, duh. You can toss it. I already got the pills."

Mental brakes. Full mental stop.

So that was the end of it. I breathed a sigh of relief, laced with a touch of disappointment. That grandbaby had been so real for a few moments. I thought of her again, snuggled into Jack's arms.

Then I began to laugh. I'm going mental. Put on the brakes!

"If you fall out of that tree and break your leg, don't come running to me."

MOTHER'S DAY

I am in one of those deep and restful slumbers, which elude me most nights, when the shrill ring of the phone on the nightstand beside my head jolts me into a half-wakeful state. My eyes seek the red glow of the digital clock, and the numbers gradually come into focus as I shake off my sleep-induced coma. 2:15 a.m. Who's hurt? Who died?

I grab the phone on the second ring. "H-hullo?" I half-whisper into the phone, partially in deference to my sleeping husband and also because my vocal chords are not yet fully functional.

"Mom?" wails the voice at the other end. It is my daughter, Leslie, a junior in college, calling me at this hour, hysterical. My heart racing, I brace myself. If she is calling, she is alive, I tell myself. Anything else, I can handle. The rest of her words come at me so quickly, intermingled with choking sobs, that I have a hard time making her out. "I'm-sorry-Mom-I'm-sorry-to-call-you-but-I'm-really-sick-and-I'm-scared-and-I-don't-know-what-to-do-I've-been-throwing-up-for-hours-and-I-can't-stop-and-I'm-by-myself-and-I'm-afraid-something-is-wrong-and…."

"Les," I interrupt, in a quiet and steady voice that is barely audible above the pounding in my head. "Slow down. I can't follow you. I need you to calm down and speak slowly." I've got a million questions. I start with the basics. "Tell me where you are right now."

"I'm at Mark's apartment." Mark? Who is Mark? Is this someone I'm supposed to know? I do a quick inventory of our recent phone conversations about passing acquaintances, friends, love interests; the name Mark isn't ringing any bells.

"And where is Mark?" I ask, feigning a familiarity with this individual and pretending that I am OK with my daughter being holed up in some guy's apartment off-campus at this hour.

"He's asleep in the other room. He was in here with me, but I just kept getting sick, so he said he'd give me privacy and he went next door to sleep in his roommate's room." She pauses to inhale. "I've been in here for a couple of hours now, and I keep throwing up. I tried drinking sips of water, but that just made me vomit more. Before I called you, I tried to wake Mark up to ask him to come back and stay with me, but I can't wake him up. I feel horrible, Mom. What should I do to make it stop?" The gasping has turned to gentle sobbing.

"Where were you before you went to Mark's?" I inquire, crossing the second question off my mental checklist.

"A few of us went out to this bar to celebrate a friend's birthday. But I swear I didn't have too much to drink, Mom. I had maybe five mixed drinks at most," she said. Note to self: In a calmer moment, let my 5' 6", 115-pound daughter know that consuming five mixed drinks in a couple of hours is *way* more than someone her age and weight can handle. But not now.

"I think I may have food poisoning, Mom. Before we went to the bar, Janey and I decided to have something to eat so that we wouldn't be drinking on an empty stomach. We each had some yogurt, but after I ate a spoonful, I noticed it had this funky taste. I let Janey try it, and she agreed it didn't taste right. So I threw most of it away."

"Then I ate part of a ham sandwich," she added.

A ham sandwich? My vegetarian daughter ate part of a *ham sandwich*?

At this point, my husband, apparently not as dead to the world as I had imagined, says in an irritated tone, "She's had too much to drink, and she probably mixed different types of alcohol. This is how she'll learn." He abruptly shifts his sleeping form in the bed, clearly annoyed at the interruption. We had gone to bed early in anticipation of our trip to

Boston the next day to pick Leslie up from school. It is the end-of-the-year pickup that requires the navigation of an oversized minivan that resembles a sixteen-wheeler and countless trips up and down the dorm stairwells to gather up all of Leslie's belongings.

"OK, so you had a small amount to eat, you went to a bar, and had drinks with friends." I meticulously gather all the pertinent facts and play them back like I am performing an investigation. "Then what?" I ask as I throw my feet off the side of the bed, stand up, and leave the bedroom to make my way down the hall to our guest bedroom so as not to disturb my husband further. No use in both of us losing precious sleep.

"I don't really remember leaving the bar, but Mark told me he'd offered to walk me back to my dorm, and when I started getting sick, he said it might make more sense for me to go back to his place instead." She hesitates for a moment. "Mom, do you think someone could have slipped something into one of my drinks?"

"Did you set your drink down at any time during the evening?" I ask. It is one of those cardinal rules we all learned about in high school classes designed to raise awareness about date rape.

"I don't know, Mom, but I'm always careful. Wait, hold on…" There is a soft thud as the phone drops to the floor and then l hear distant gagging, the unmistakable sound of dry heaves. In an attempt to distract myself, I suddenly recall a holiday concert performed by the children's choir at church. I see nine-year-old Leslie standing in front of the group, wearing the maroon velvet dress with the ecru lace Peter Pan collar, singing her solo in a clear and confident voice. I once again feel the tears welling up in my eyes as I watch and listen, with pride and awe, as this sweet angel sings fearlessly before the congregation. And now, that same sweet face, a bit more elongated and with better-defined features perhaps, is violently twisted as her body struggles to expel whatever poison she has put into it.

How did we get here? I wonder. Is this the education our $50,000 college tuition check buys? Then I hear footsteps, and Leslie is on the phone again. "Sorry 'bout that, Mom. Anyway, I'm always careful about holding onto my drinks when we're at a bar," she responds, picking up right where she left off. OK, so she remembers the rule. I feel a small degree of comfort. And she is speaking lucidly, I suddenly notice, which increases my comfort level another notch.

I keep Leslie engaged in dialogue, hoping that as we talk, she will continue to calm down and the nausea will eventually subside. After a few more minutes of idle chatter, her responses come more slowly.

"Leslie," I say, checking to see if she is still responsive.

"Huh?" she responds from a distance. The phone is no longer to her ear. I hear soft, regular breathing.

"Can you hear me?" I say softly.

"Uh-huh," I get in response after a short silence. She seems to be falling asleep. That's good, I think.

"Leslie," I repeat, "I think you're falling asleep, honey. I'm going to hang up now. You should do the same." No response. I hang up, reluctantly, and then immediately realize I have just cut off the lifeline to the most precious being in my life.

I sit on the floor of the guestroom, suddenly shivering in the cold night air. I head back to our bedroom, slide under the covers, and lean against my husband's warm body, trying to match my breathing pattern to his, hoping to return to my earlier slumber. But while my body starts to relax, my mind is fully alert. What if she falls unconscious? What if she gets sick in her sleep and chokes on her own vomit? What if this Mark character takes advantage of her in her current state? What if she is under the influence of drugs and she never wakes up again? I toss and turn until night dissolves into early daybreak, and then it is time to leave for our trip.

On the way to Boston, I check my phone frequently to see if Leslie has called. Now, in the light of day, the horrors I played out in my head during the wee hours of the night feel overblown. I think, with a smile, at how amazing it is that I have a twenty-one-year-old daughter who feels comfortable calling me in the middle of the night in a compromised state, something I never could have done with my parents. For a moment, I swell with pride, but then immediately wonder if it means she is overly dependent on me. I sit in silent worry and then instinctively glance over at my husband, who has his eyes on the road and is humming to the music on the radio. He senses my eyes on him and turns to look at me.

"What?"

"Nothing," I say with a sigh, turning my head back to the road ahead. He wouldn't understand. Oh, how much simpler it is to be a dad.

Two hours later, we pull up to Leslie's dorm, and my hands shake slightly as I call her cell phone.

She picks up almost immediately. "Hi, there," she says in a chipper voice. "You here already?" She joins us downstairs and gives us each a quick hug. I glance at her face for signs of wear. Nothing. No dark circles, no ashen skin, just as beautiful and glowing as ever. Yet I feel like I have aged at least ten years overnight.

The box brigade begins, and before we know it, the car is stuffed to the gills, and we leave for home. It is a beautiful, warm, sunny spring day. My head hurts from lack of sleep, but my mood lifts as I realize we have successfully skirted disaster. Fifteen minutes into the trip, I turn around and see Leslie curled up against the pillows and other bedding jammed beside her in the backseat, sound asleep.

"I guess she needs her beauty rest after a tough night," my husband says with a hint of sarcasm in his voice.

"I suppose," I reply. My eyelids are heavy, craving sleep as well. I lean my head against the window and let the cool glass soothe the slight throbbing in my head.

"Oh, I almost forgot," my husband adds as he extends his arm and gently strokes my cheek. "Happy Mother's Day."

"Go get lost someplace where I can find you!"

TEMPEST ON A TEACUP

*I*t started out as one of those great family getaways—a car trip from our home in Colorado to visit my brother in Phoenix, two days in Sedona, and on to the Grand Canyon before heading home.

Our twin boys were eight—a perfect age for an adventurous vacation. Like typical siblings, they have always had their ups and downs and ins and outs with each other. A car trip always heightens some of the close-quarters' tensions. And, while they would never admit it, they also have a deep connection, deeper than standard siblings—it's the twin thing.

We arrived in the area of the Grand Canyon at about 2 p.m. Did I mention the close-quarters' tension that builds around day six of a car trip? Everyone was a little hot and tired from the long ride from Sedona. When we pulled up to the first visitor parking lot as we entered the Grand Canyon area, we were all a little disappointed—OK, well let me just say, downright cranky.

"Is this all there is?" We all muttered and grumped to our miserable, tired selves. It was a parking lot in a treed area with no famous attraction in sight. We could see, however, other visitors leaving their cars and walking through the trees. With the kids in tow (more like in drag), we got out of the car and walked toward the edge of the parking lot.

Through the far side of the tree line, I gasped in awe. The heavens opened up to the most spectacular wonder I have ever seen on this Earth. In my travels, I have seen many of the marvels this world has to offer—from the great pyramids of Egypt to the fjords of Norway. For me, nothing matched the brilliant colors and cavernous sight in front of me.

In a visitor outlook area, we perched in timeless fascination taking in the panoramic beauty of the teacup. I felt a tremendous need to latch onto a visual metaphor that could fathom what I was seeing, and it came to me then—a beautiful and fragile teacup. Looking into a teacup, especially one that was passed down from, let's say, a great-great grandmother, one can see the delicate cracks and lines of time, the warmth from the water that passed through its cup over the years, and the shadings and colorations left behind.

What struck me even more than the bowl of this grand cup was the rim. As I gazed out across the canyon, I was particularly mesmerized by the thin edge that separated the bowl from the world that it was stuck to.

My feet were touching that same world, but felt far from securely stuck. Frozen in awe and fear, I was afraid that moving even ever-so-slightly might cause the earth to come apart under my feet. My only hope for survival, if that should happen, would be turning my slippage into my best Olympic swan dive off the rim, ending with a backstroke glide through warm tea at the bottom of the teacup. It being highly unlikely that I could pull that off, I stood still on terra firma and enjoyed the view.

When something is breathtaking, it literally takes your breath away. So I admit to concentrating on breathing and losing any conscious sight of the boys for minutes or hours, who knows?

It was not until one son tugged at my sleeve, "How much longer are we going to stand here?" that I breathed in and, ever so slowly, pulled back into the here and now. I looked at my face staring back at me—my face in the body of a little boy, who was obviously annoyed.

Who are you again? I wondered, still dazed. Ah, right—mother, son. My brain finally shook off the celestial seasoning that had lulled me away from all earthly responsibility.

I suggested we walk a little bit down the path that goes around the rim, but then I stopped so abruptly that I almost felt the ever-so-fragile terra firma quiver under my feet.

"Where's your brother?" An ever-so-tiny quiver trembled inside my body.

"How am I supposed to know?" scowled that eight-year-old face of mine, even more annoyed. He was not envisioning teacups or standing frozen in breathless awe. He simply didn't know where his brother was.

The visitor area was large and crowded, full of tourists and park rangers. We walked through seemingly endless rooms and exhibits for five, ten, fifteen minutes, scanning to locate small, unaccompanied children. My heart sank to the bottom of the canyon in my stomach. Nowhere in sight was the second copy of this little boy, no second small-boy version of me with curly corn silk hair, last seen wearing tan shorts and a pale blue T-shirt looking identical to his other half. Remember, just a few minutes ago I described how, when something is breathtaking, it takes your breath away? Well, now I felt like I could not breathe, and it had nothing to do with beauty and everything to do with raw fear at the bottom of my belly, rising to the rim of my eyes that began to tear up.

Back at the canyon, I saw my husband balancing along the teacup rim. "Good. Phew!" I assumed that I could now breathe that cleansing sigh of relief; surely the other twin was with him.

But the sigh quickly caught in my throat, cutting off any possible means to continue breathing. Tom was alone.

The tea must have swirled and tilted in the bottom of the

cup as the only explanation for that feeling of the slippery slope of my conscious mind closing in on me. The last thing my husband recalled his most adoring fan saying was, "This is boring."

"Maybe he's in the bathroom." While my husband strode down the walkway to check if our missing little man had gone to the restrooms, I continued to scan the visitor area. Having just experienced the beauty that takes your breath away, all I could think was, "Keep breathing. Don't panic." My little face inside that little boy's body looking up at me needed an "all's right with the world explanation for all this" from me. He needed to see me stay calm.

Ever since he was very young, this boy saw monsters under the bed and scary closet creepers. I could tell just by looking at that face that his childhood fears were crawling up the side of the cup, just waiting to pounce on him, too.

Frankly, I was envisioning the monsters and the creeps that could have abducted my other darling little boy, taking him away from us forever. Now I felt the ground truly shaking. It was anything but terra firma beneath me, and the cup was swirling me sick as I screamed inside my head, *why* did we come here? Nothing is right about this. It is not a beautiful teacup; it's a dirty, ugly sinkhole sucking everything that matters to me out of my life and down its drain to hell.

I saw my husband returning from the restroom path with no curly towhead in tow. Now, it was terror on the teacup and time to panic. I frantically searched for park rangers who were in over-abundance just a few minutes before but who now were nowhere in sight. Where are you? Damn it, don't you understand? My son is missing, and we need help! My silent scream echoed off the fragile hold I had on my heart, shattering it like Grandma's old china.

My husband headed down the path that goes around the rim and, unbeknownst to me, kept peering over the side of the rim, calling out into the cup below. More time passed; my anxiety grew. The sun was sinking lower. Darkness would cause the temperature to drop into the forties or lower out here in the desert. I could not bear to think of it.

Full panic as expressed by an eight-year-old echoed off of the fragile cup, threatening to crack any hold I had on composure and calm. "Why did we come here? Whose idea was this? This was the stupidest thing we have ever done." Finally, at the top of his spiraling terror, he screamed into the stillness of the air and echo of the cup, "I can't go through life without my twin!" Twin…twin…twin…twin echoed tauntingly off the canyon walls.

My husband headed to the car to get his cell phone to call 911. When he re-emerged through the trees, the one boy and I were holding onto each other, weeping and wishing we could turn back time.

Blinded by our fright, it took some unquantifiable amount of frozen time to thaw enough to realize that the half is once again a whole. A whole! A whole! A whole! The word echoed through my heart.

Yes, he had been bored. But no, he had not been bored enough to do a Lipton leap or a Celestial swan dive. He had followed someone he thought was Pop down the rim path. It was a while before he realized it was some other six-foot string bean in canvas shorts and a faded baseball cap. He had gotten disoriented navigating his way back but eventually found the car, where he had been waiting for us.

***

The twins are going on eighteen now. They have continued to have their ups and downs and ins and outs with each other over the years. And, while it goes unspoken, I know that from the rim of their skin to the bottom cup of their hearts, they remember the day that they didn't have to learn to live without their other half, and they are as grateful for being whole as I am. It's the twin thing.

Kid: "I'm trying!"

Mom: "Yes, you're very trying."

THE SKI TRIP

The high school ski trip was at the end of the week.
We'd been shopping and packing; the skis were all tweaked.

On the big day, I gave my usual spiel:
"Make good choices—that's the deal."

"I don't want any calls—no drugs, alcohol, or sex."
So when the phone rang early morn, we were perplexed.

On the line was a crying and hysterical child,
Explaining, while sobbing, how the prior night had gone wild.

A swim in the pool had turned into strip poker.
She'd no intention of stripping—oh, she's quite the joker!

What on earth was my pretty girl thinking?
She'd made this decision without even blinking.

I thought my instructions were loud and clear.
What part of "make good choices" did she not hear?

She told me she was sorry and had been up all night crying.
I wasn't fully awake and just hoped she wasn't lying.

Chaperones made them call; but it wasn't "send home" trouble.
When she got home we'd discuss it, and sift through the rubble.

I'm sure she hung up feeling quite relieved.
But when Dad heard the story, boy, was he peeved!

As we lay in bed talking, unable to fall back to sleep,
She was skiing the slopes of Loon's most steep.

She's not even home and has ruined our day.
And what's she out doing? Having a fun day of play!

So, the decision was made—we were New Hampshire bound,
Wondering, when we got there, exactly what would be found?

Our day shouldn't have to be spent like this.
We should be at home in empty nester bliss.

But, what kind of parents would we really be,
If we just closed our eyes and pretended not to see?

She was the one who hadn't thought things through.
To our convictions, we should remain true.

I certainly knew it was the right thing to do.
So why I felt so uneasy, I had not a clue.

I didn't want to embarrass her in front of her friends.
But that's the difficult message a lesson sends.

The kids buzzed through the door like a swarm of bees.
From the look on her face—she was not pleased.

She knew we'd come a long way and gave us a hug.
Her dad started crying. I wanted to crawl under a rug.

In her heart, she knew what she had done was wrong.
As parents, we knew we had to remain strong.

"Go pack your things. We'll wait for you here."
There was no turning back now, that was clear.

A chaperone confirmed we'd made the right move.
For our lovely daughter, we had something to prove.

The car ride home was spent talking things out.
She only half-understood what the fuss was about.

Our contention remained as originally voiced.
She finally agreed her actions weren't her best choice.

We knew that as the learning experiences amassed,
This awkward situation would also surely pass.

We can look back at it now and muster a smile.
But for me and her dad, that took quite awhile.

Each of our children has pulled one thing or another.
I guess it was just my kid's turn to embarrass her mother.

JUST ORDINARY MOMS

"What do I look like, a bank?"

TELL IT LIKE IT IS—A TRILOGY

Being a mother can be an unlimited source of entertainment.
Children have a talent for saying just how it is.

All That Glitters

*O*ur busy and self-reliant preschool daughter, Sydney, and I were traveling to Florida. Dad was to meet us there for well-deserved rest and relaxation. Sydney, an only child, had jam-packed her girlie pink and purple roller suitcase with an abundance of amusing items that she had chosen independently: Amazon rain forest puzzles, favorite rhyming story books, and most importantly, all sorts of necessities that her doll, Sally, would need to travel to a sub-tropical paradise.

Apparently, Sally required just as many items as Sydney did: bathing suits, sundresses, a floppy straw hat, and the fuzzy, worn blankie that always kept the doll and its owner comfortable and secure.

The roller suitcase zipper was strong but showed signs of slight strain as Sydney guided it carefully behind her, weaving through an endless stream of people while diligently following me in the busy international airport. Glancing back, I could see her long, flaxen pigtails swaying back and forth and her sweet, wide-eyed face tilted up, looking at the endless parade of interesting faces in the airport.

The Miami airport bustled with diverse cultures. People, especially women, were dressed in a vast variety of styles and colors and, at times, were in stark contrast to one another. We saw women with burkas covering their faces; women in shorts, long pants, and Capri-style trousers; and women with studded earrings lined up one side of the ear's cartilage, only to have them turn their heads and reveal another array trailing up the other ear. Many ladies wore brightly colored, flowing shirtsleeves or sleeveless blouses, quite a change from our typical New England polo shirts and oxfords. Body types ranged from the youthfully slender to the lumpy, centennially mature, with skin types varying from sun-leathered to soft as a newborn's cheek.

The men had contrasting styles, too. Whether wearing Tommy Bahama prints or dark business suits, many carried cases that housed items such as computers or electronic gadgets to allow them to stay connected to the latest news, while others enjoyed the simplicity of a daily printed newspaper.

From fanciful to playful to the everyday mundane, the scene was surely eye-catching for a small child. Most of all, the glitz and glamour of the mountains of gold adorning both the men and women was a sight to behold.

Gold was everywhere! It sparkled, catching the sun's rays through a window and bouncing off its shiny, metallic finish. Handbags, bracelets, belts, earrings, blouses, necklaces, pierced studs, rings, hair barrettes, and even shoes were laced with shiny gold material. Some men even had several heavy gold chains around their necks. Although I could tell that much of the gold was simply costume jewelry, it was obvious that all this glistening caught Sydney's attention and put her in an enamored state of pure, magical awe as we arrived at the assigned gate.

Sydney chattered with her well-loved doll cradled in the crook of her arm. "Sally, there are lots of people here, so you need to pay attention or you will get lost, and I will be sad," Sydney logically explained, as earnestly as any mother would.

"All these people are grown-ups and don't need diapers like you do. They are getting on planes to go to places you cannot go to in a car," Sydney continued as she began to feed the faux baby bottle to the doll.

Then, in a whispering voice so as to assure confidentially to Sally, she leaned in very close to the doll and offered the most vital information yet: "These ladies must be very *rich*."

I sat comfortably in the chair anticipating the boarding call, listening to Sydney's chatter as people milled around the gate and walked past us in both directions. Indeed, I knew Sydney was right—these people in the airport obviously had some wealth because they could afford plane tickets to all sorts of international destinations.

Sydney's perspective was a little different. She looked up at me with a face so innocent, yet laced with the wisdom of discovery reaffirmed, and said, "There must be a lot of rich people here, Mommy. Look, that lady is *wearing* gold." Captivated, she pointed to what must have seemed the most striking sight she had ever seen: a beautiful young woman in a head-to-toe gold lamé dress that shimmered as she walked—a fairy-tale princess come to life.

In her innocence, Sydney believed that gold buttons, gold belts, gold straps, gold earrings, gold chains (real or otherwise), and most of all, gold lamé, were the ultimate sign of wealth. Banks, investment accounts, mansions, health and happiness—no matter. Just gold, glittering gold.

I knew that someday we would have a different conversation. But for now, who could argue with her view of the world? Children say it just like it is.

Locks of Love

*I*n a school culture that promotes diversity, tolerance, and empathy among all students, Sydney was a fifth-grader at one of our town's two elementary schools. Her class had a nice balance of boys and girls. Children at this age can be very opinionated and test each other's friendships, but there was only warm interaction amongst this particular group.

Long, golden tresses that fell to her slender waist complemented Sydney's sapphire eyes, framed with dark lashes. Her hair was usually braided or in a ponytail so it was out of her face for academics and sports activities. The summer was rapidly approaching, and Sydney decided she would cut her hair for easier care.

She had also learned about a program called Locks of Love, a charity that makes hairpieces or wigs for children who are undergoing medical treatment that results in hair loss. If you have hair that is twelve inches long or more, you can cut it and donate it to the Locks of Love organization. Sydney had known older girls who had participated in the program, and, with our blessing, she decided to have her gorgeous long hair cut and donated to this wonderful cause.

It was a dazzling spring day, the kind of day made for celebrating the onset of sunny skies and warm temperatures after a long, chilly New England winter. We headed out to the local salon and asked to participate in the Locks of Love program. The hairdresser put Sydney's hair in a neat ponytail that cascaded down her back, curling at the very tip. There was just the right amount of room between the binding elastic and her head and, with one giant cut of the sharp, steel, scissor blades, the saffron ponytail was in the hands of the hairdresser.

Sydney looked in the mirror, smiled, and asked, "How will my hair be styled?"

The haircut resulted in a chic bob designed right around her face, and she was transformed into a different look altogether—a look that made her feel new and fresh but still look like an amiable, adorable child. We mailed the clipped ponytail to Locks of Love.

Sydney went to school the following day, and her female classmates gathered around her. "Why did you get your hair cut so short?" Sydney explained her logical reasoning—to help sick children—and they all chattered about how it made her look so different and would be so easy to care for.

The teacher offered brief praise in front of the class, saying, "Sydney, you have done a noble and selfless act, one that I am sure another child will benefit from. You might have made it possible for another child somewhere to attend school without being embarrassed because she has lost all her hair. Good for you!" Sydney smiled, and the day's classroom activities continued.

During the day's revered recess, the boys began to taunt

Sydney and call her names: "Ugly." "Dork." "Stupid." Undeterred, Sydney went back to class, impervious to the unkind name-calling and remarks. When Sydney got home that afternoon, she never mentioned any of this; it was business as usual with a snack and homework.

The following day at school, it started again. One of the boys cornered her: "Why did you go and get all your hair cut off?"

"I did it because I want to help sick children who are about our age but have lost their hair. They are going to make a wig out of my hair that sick kids can wear."

Another boy chimed in, advising her that cutting off her hair was a "big mistake" and she should have "left it alone."

Later that same day, there was a classroom activity organized by the teacher whereby the students were put into teams. Sydney's partners were some of the same boys she had gotten unkind hair reviews from, and when the group received its instructions on the activity, the boys took the overt opportunity to once again inform Sydney that her hair was "awful looking."

The teacher, monitoring the group's activity, immediately pulled the boys from the room into the hallway. Once there, she spoke to them about the reason Sydney cut her hair. The teacher informed the boys the cause was a "noble" one: a cause that helped sick children, children whose opportunities might not include going to school and learning because they were so sick for so long, children who might be saved from embarrassment by the wigs. "Furthermore, even if someone's appearance changes, they are still the same person." The boys, somewhat wide-eyed and probably fearing a consequence, nodded, and the teacher sent them back into the classroom to finish their activity.

At home, Sydney never uttered a word to us about that day or the ridicule she had experienced. The three of us chatted together over dinner as usual. We retired for the night, and the next day dawned.

Because it was the end of the school year, there was an awards assembly for the school and parents. I had been informed that Sydney would be receiving at least one award. Proudly, I watched as Sydney and her friends received honors for playing instruments in the band, as well as athletic and academic awards. Surmising that the ceremony was about to close, I scanned the auditorium's layout to plan a route so I could perhaps catch a glimpse of Sydney as she returned to her classroom for eventual dismissal.

I was barely paying attention as the principal spoke: "Today we have one final award that is for a very noble cause, a cause that involved an activity outside of our classroom walls, but one we can all learn from. Many of you have heard about the program called Locks of Love, and we have a student who has participated in the program and given of herself. This award goes to Sydney Benson who has cut her hair so that sick children who have lost their own hair will have a chance to look normal even though they are receiving medical treatment due to an illness. Sydney, would you please come forward?" Sydney beamed, and my heart swelled with pride. I was proud of her both for having chosen to participate in this charitable act and to be so happy about doing it.

As the ceremony came to an end, I managed to catch Sydney's eye and give her a wink, indicating that I would see her at home later. As we all exited the building, parents chatted, "What a nice way to end the school year," and how we all were looking forward to the summer break.

Sydney's teacher caught my attention and called me over. It was then that she told me the story of the boys in the class and their cruel reactions to Sydney's changed appearance. I was stunned by the judgments that the boys had passed on a girl, simply because she had become less attractive in their eyes. Where was their respect for someone who was willing to make a personal sacrifice, so that others may feel more attractive and accepted?

When Sydney arrived home, I asked her about the boys' comments. She confirmed they had been "mean."

I looked into her eyes, "Are you sure you are OK, honey?"

She smiled. "Mom, boys will be boys. We need them as friends and on our teams. But really, I think they just don't like change."

That is so true, honey, I thought. You said it *exactly* like it is.

Payback Time

*B*reezily I passed by the shiny granite breakfast counter on my way to the foyer and then stopped, my steps paralyzed by the sight of the neat piles of cash. Stacked in three precise groups were ones, tens, and twenty-dollar bills. The stack of singles reached many inches high. Where did all this money come from? More importantly, whose was it?

"Mom? Mom? Where are you?" my teenage daughter yelled from the stairway.

"I am right here in the kitchen looking at a gazillion dollars on the counter," I offered cautiously.

"Yeah, yeah, yeah, I need for you to get me a deposit envelope and on our way out to the store, make a stop at the ATM and put the money in your bank account," came the plan of the moment.

"Honey, where did all this cash come from? And you probably don't realize it, but the ATM is unable to take thick piles of cash like this." I could not resist reaching to count the money while still in amazement at the Washingtons, Hamiltons, and Jacksons staring me down. How much did this kid have? I knew she had received money at celebratory occasions like birthdays and from her part-time job, but most of the time, it seemed like school, seasonal sports, and friends took up her time. Obviously, she had been working more hours than I realized.

"I have some checks, too," came the voice from the hallway.

"Sydney, we need to talk about this. First, I will be happy to deposit the money and checks in my account, but then we need to get our act together. I know and understand about the paychecks, but the stacks of cash need explaining."

In the mature world of the teenager, there is very limited explaining and far more focus on convenience.

Sydney entered the room. "It's simple, Mom. You can just give me money out of the ATM when I need it for shopping or stuff."

"Whoa, pull the reins in on this pony, babe," I exclaimed. "Comingling funds and then asking for money presents a whole new set of issues. There is 'your' accounting and 'my' accounting, for example. This also introduces a tax event your father needs to know about. Also, you should be saving for future expenses."

"Mom, what are you talking about? Taxes, savings, future expenses—this is all too complicated. Just hold the money for me."

I stood for a moment looking at my young daughter who obviously knew how to earn money, and lots of it. I carefully counted the cash and estimated the few paychecks. We were looking at close to a thousand dollars.

"Sydney, I understand the paycheck stubs, but all this cash—where did all the ones come from?"

"Tips from the golf course gig. Remember?"

Geez, I thought. Who knew a fun day helping at a charity golf outing could be so profitable?

My mind was clicking away, processing a multitude of thoughts. I could already see that mixing funds in my bank account would only lead to exclamations of, "I thought I had more money than that!" and "Is that all that's left? Are you sure?" Next, there would be tax implications. If the kid kept working at this pace, and the summer had yet to come, she would exceed the exemption amount allowed by the IRS for student earnings, and that would cause her father a tax accounting nightmare. Even more complex was the idea of saving for future college books and expenses.

After a trip to the drugstore, we visited the bank teller and deposited her funds into my account for safekeeping. I handed Sydney the deposit slip. "Here, hold onto this for your records." I watched while she crumpled it into the back pocket of her jeans. That receipt would never see the inside of a desk drawer; it was surely destined for the washer/dryer battleground, where all tiny but important pieces of paper go to die.

I slipped into the bank manager's office and inquired

about student bank accounts. "Not a problem, Mrs. Benson. We would be happy to set an account up for Sydney. All you have to do is co-sign since she is under eighteen. She will have her own ATM card, and she can deposit and direct her funds independently. Come back when you have these pieces of information," he said, handing me a list of required documentation.

Am I rushing a process? My baby is growing up fast, and I am promoting progressive responsibilities. But is this the right thing to do? Am I making things too complicated for a kid?

"Come back when you both have time to sit down with us for a little while. We will get everything set up then," the manager said.

How matter of fact—just like a banking transaction.

"Thank you," I said, relieved but still unsure. "We will be back in a few days."

On the ride home, I reflected that the banking portion of this endeavor would be rather easy compared to the father/daughter discussion yet to take place.

I spoke to my husband that night and explained the financial events of the day. As the CEO and CFO of our home, he viewed the situation as requiring even more structure.

"If she continues to earn at this rate, I project there will be additional taxes beyond what is already reflected in these paystubs. She will need to open a 401(k) IRA to avoid that, and we need to tell her that the responsibility of college books and some other college expenses is hers and hers alone. She should save some money on basic principle, as well."

I knew this would be a tough sell to Sydney, but it was a start in the right direction. Sure enough, upon hearing this news, Sydney was shell-shocked. Her father retreated to the downstairs office computer to set up a spreadsheet to chart earnings, his job done.

Conspiratorially, Sydney tried a flanking maneuver around her Dad. "Mom, I just think it would be easier for you to hold onto my money for me."

"Lamb chop," I said, trying to woo her, "you want control over your money, and the bank can help you with that. I know it sounds like a lot for someone your age, but I will go with you and set things up, and you will be much happier for it, believe me."

Disenchanted with the family chat, Sydney left the room, mumbling, "Parents…."

The following week, armed with Social Security numbers, passports, and my check made out for the amount previously deposited, we scooted off to the bank. The manager escorted us to his office.

"Sydney, your mom tells me you want to open an account with us and have your very own ATM card," he said.

"Well, *she* wants me to," Sydney retorted.

"You should take this action as a compliment from your mom. She believes you are responsible and can handle your own money. I wish more parents were as confident in their children as your mom is in you. Of course, your mom has to co-sign with you."

"That's good, I guess. If I knew what the co-signing was all about," Sydney murmured.

"Did you bring your pieces of identification?"

Sydney turned them over to the manager, along with my check for her funds to open the account.

"Now, Sydney, you will get an ATM card. I know you will remember that in order to get money out of the machine, you have to make deposits first," the manager said, smiling and winking at her. "Would you like checks as well?"

Sydney looked at him and then at me. It was a look of bewilderment, no doubt wondering why she was even sitting in that chair.

"Checks? What would I need checks for? I am not paying anyone. I don't even know how to fill one out."

But you sure like *cashing* them! I thought with sarcasm.

The bank manager glanced at me and began a very logical explanation of the need for checks. Two seconds later and without a blink, Sydney said, "No, thank you." Well, at least she was being polite, I noted wryly.

"Not a problem. You can always order them in the future

if you need them," he concluded. "Now, let me get things going here." He left with the information and returned shortly with papers for this and papers for that. Sydney and I signed them all.

"Now about the 401(k) IRA account. Do you have the amount that you wish to open with?"

"I wouldn't have a clue," she answered in a teenage voice that was not only tentative, but also actually a little frightened. "All these ABCs and numbers, it is like I am back in pre-school and have no idea what you are talking about." She continued grinning but appeared very unsure as to where all her hard-earned cash was going.

I stepped in and told the manager to open the 401(k) IRA in the pre-determined amount set by Sydney's father and handed him the check I had already written.

Again, the bank manager left with the check and paperwork.

Sydney looked at me, with pleading eyes and her voice almost trembling, "Mom, how am I supposed to do all this stuff? All these letters and numbers? I'm just a kid!"

"Welcome to the financial world," I said. "And now you know why you may need checks soon. For example, to pay me back the money I just shelled out for your retirement account."

"Pay you *back*—for what?"

"Well, that was *my* money we just used to open the IRA

account. We will talk about it after we leave; let's just get this done now."

At this point, she would have done anything to get out of the massive, overstuffed wing chair that practically swallowed up her willowy frame. The manager returned, handed her a packet with all her goodies, and we said our good-byes.

Once in the car, Sydney turned to me and said, "Pay for what? How much will I have left? Why?"

"There are a lot of expenses in your future, and keeping track of your money will let *you* understand what you can and cannot afford to do," I explained. I could already see the wheels beginning to turn.

She turned toward me and said with a pout, "It was supposed to be for shopping."

Oh yes, children certainly do say it like it is.

"Go put on a sweater. I'm freezing!"

LABOR DAYS

*B*efore we get to the labor part, a little bit about pregnancy. I was huge. I mean, looking like a whale! My first son was due in June, and I had gained forty pounds and I had only weighed 110 pounds to begin with. I really did not think I was eating that much, but I guess I was.

It never bothered me when strangers touched my stomach. I was so excited. I had a little bit of nausea at the beginning and a fair amount of heartburn; I ate Tums constantly (and food as well, apparently).

At one point, because I was so big, the doctor who was examining me thought I might be having twins. She scheduled an ultrasound (back then they were not routine). I told my husband about the possibility of twins, and he did not believe me because back on April Fool's Day, I had told him that the doctor said I was having twins, just to be funny.

Well, now it was not so funny.

The doctor did the ultrasound and found just one baby. The doctor also asked if I wanted to know the sex. "No," I firmly replied. Just for the record, I do not approve when people know the sex of the baby. I always thought that was half the fun of it.

I did not care if I had a boy or a girl; I just wanted a fair-haired baby. My hair is light, and my husband's is very dark. I wanted to *win* that one. I used to joke and say that if the baby did not have golden hair, I would send him back. (He came out blond, so we are OK.)

The kid was due on June 17. I am giving all of you who are pregnant a bit of advice: Do not tell anyone your real due date—you must add at least a week. Seriously, this is the best advice I can give you. I was inundated with phone calls every day after June 17th, asking why I had not had the baby yet. Family, friends, neighbors, and even the President of the United States called to find the whereabouts of this unborn child (well, not the President; I made that up).

I worked up until the day he was born. With your first child, unless you are having complications and your doctor won't let you work, there is no need to take any time off before the baby is due. You already have the tiny new clothes washed, the room adorably decorated, the lotions all lined up, and diapers neatly stacked. You have cleaned the house eight dozen times (known as "nesting"). If you take time off, there will be nothing to do but wait, and that just makes the time go by more slowly.

I called my boss one night, a few days after my due date, because my stomach was bothering me.

She laughed at the other end. "I guess you'll be having the baby tomorrow."

"No, I think I am coming down with the flu." I went to bed about 8:00 p.m., not unusual in those late pregnancy days. I woke up in the wee hours with pains in my stomach and went to the bathroom, ready to barf from the flu and then realized—this was *labor*. Doesn't that word just make you tired?

Did I wake my husband up immediately? No. I ironed. Why I ironed, I have no idea, but that is what I have done now for three labors. By the way, I hate to iron. But it has helped me get through three labors. I ironed through contractions for several hours, took a shower, woke my husband up at 6:30 a.m. and said, "Time to go to the hospital."

In the emergency room, everyone was just full of advice. The admitting nurse said since it was my first, it would be about twenty-four hours before I had the baby. When you are in terrible pain, this is not what you want to hear. Someone else said, "Walk around to encourage the labor," and another nurse advised me to lie on this side or that to ease the pain.

They admitted me to the official Labor and Delivery

Wing, and I announced I wanted no pain medicine because I had opted to have natural childbirth (not smart, ladies). The doctor examined me; I was five to six centimeters dilated. Yes! I thought. It won't be long now. The nurses decided to give me an enema, preferring "babies only" on the delivery table. An enema is an extremely uncomfortable thing anyway, but when you are in labor, it is awful.

The contractions were getting closer and closer and were very painful. They were about two minutes apart. You could have peeled me off the ceiling, I was in so much pain. I looked over at my husband for support. Where did he go?

I looked down. "What the hell are you doing on the floor?"

"Sir, sir, have some juice," the nurse said.

Hey, what about *me?* I need the attention right now, not him. I am the one having the baby, and I am going to deliver any second now.

The doctor came in to examine me. It was 10 a.m. "Oh, wonderful! You are progressing well. You are now a little more than seven centimeters, so it should only be about three or four hours now."

"Are you f-ing kidding me? Four more hours—I don't think so." I hissed at him. "I am no longer participating in natural childbirth. I want the drugs, *all* the drugs you can possibly give me, every single one of the ones you have been trying to give me since I arrived, and I want them *now!*"

A lovely potion flowed through my veins. I fell into a warm, relaxing pool of water. I think it was a hot tub of some sort. How they got the hot tub into the room and onto my bed, I have no idea, but I thought I should thank them later, as this was simply heavenly.

I relaxed. A contraction came, and I just drifted.

But something felt funny down there. "I think the baby is falling out. We need the doctor!"

"It's OK, dear, he will be back in a few minutes."

"*No, no!* I need to push! We need him *now.*"

The doctor returned. He was patronizing. "You've got four hours to go, remember? But if it will make you feel better, I will recheck you." He took a peek, and broke into a sweat. "Well, now! Oh, yes, just as I thought. You are fully dilated. I think you should push now."

I followed his advice because, after all, he was the expert.

One, two, three, maybe four pushes, assisted by an episiotomy, and out popped son number one, a beautiful, blue-eyed, fair-haired boy, at 10:35 a.m. on June 20th.

The doctor turned to my husband to congratulate him and asked, "Would you like to cut the umbilical cord?"

"No, thanks," was his quick reply. Uh-oh, I thought. He's headed for the floor again.

***

The next pregnancy was uneventful. I felt great, ate well, and once again put on about forty pounds. Some people said it was a boy because I was carrying high. Some people said it was a girl because I was carrying low.

I kept working so I could maximize my time off after the baby was born. My first son was just a toddler, so I was already tired. Tired from working, tired from mommying. I pretty much went to bed at the same time as the toddler.

At 2 a.m. a few days after my due date, I awoke with stomach pains (do you see a pattern?). So I ironed.

Once again, I woke my husband up at 6:30 in the morning. I called the doctor, who said, "Well, I guess you could go to the hospital. But you do not sound like you are in labor."

"Yes, I am. My stomach has been hurting for four hours," I insisted.

"Go ahead. I'll meet you there, and we'll move things along if need be," was his reply. Obviously, he was the expert.

The whole ride there, I kept praying that I really was in labor. You hear so many stories of women getting to the hospital and then being sent home. Or worse, being hooked up to monitors and tubes for hours and hours, even days and days. No, thank you!

The resident examined me because my doctor was not there yet. I was excited to hear that I was seven centimeters dilated! Yes, it was labor, all right.

The nurse came with that dreaded enema again. As soon as I finished in the bathroom, I screamed to my husband that the baby was coming out. "Get the nurse, quick!" Where is the call bell when you need it? Apparently ripped out of the wall by a previous mother in labor.

"Get up on the bed," the nurse ordered when she saw me crumpled over.

"No. I can't. I can't get up there." The bed might as well have been Mt. Everest.

"You must."

"I won't!"

"You will!"

"I can't!" She and my husband hoisted me onto the bed. That could not have been easy. The nurse glanced under the gown and ran out of the room.

"Where the hell are you going?"

"We need a doctor, stat!" she screamed into the hallway.

The resident rushed in, took one look, and said, "Push! You are going to have a baby!"

Oh really? You are telling me something I don't know? Well, you're the expert. Or will be one day.

One, two, out came our second boy, crying so loudly for such a little thing.

"Hello," said my husband, snuggling him close. The child quieted instantly.

I was in the hospital a total of thirty-five minutes before our son was born. I do not recommend this.

Awhile later, when my doctor walked in and I was holding a baby, his eyes practically popped out of his head. Funny thing is, we still got a bill from the doctor's office. After all, he was the expert.

***

With my third pregnancy, I still felt great although a lot more tired from working nights. Oh, and having a five-year-old and a three-year-old.

I did stop working a week before my due date, just to get some sleep before the baby arrived. Having a baby in December is the best way to get you organized for the holidays. I had sent out all of our Christmas cards already and had all of the gifts bought and mostly wrapped before Thanksgiving.

My husband plays poker in the neighborhood on Friday nights. "Are you sure it is OK if I go?" he asked for the third time.

"What are you going to do, sit and stare at me sitting and staring at you? You're only five minutes away, and it might be your last chance for a while. Go!"

I finished wrapping the last few presents and shuffled down into the basement, where I hid the Santa Claus gifts. Suddenly, whoosh! Wetness began flowing down my legs. So this is what it feels like when your water breaks and you are not lying down. Niagara Falls.

I looked around for a towel or some laundry, but closer at hand was one of the kid's stuffed animals (no, not a Christmas gift). With Teddy Bear shoved between my legs, I waddled up the stairs.

I called the doctor's office, and they told me to get to the hospital immediately. There were not any contractions yet, so I felt no need to rush. I called my husband at the neighbor's, took a shower, and called another neighbor to come stay with the kids. She arrived in three minutes. My husband, on the other hand, was nowhere in sight.

I rang the poker house again. "Where are you?"

"Just finishing up a hand." It was yet another half an hour before he got home. I briefly considered beaning him with the iron.

We arrived at the hospital two hours after my water broke. The doctor was alarmed, especially after last time's quick delivery. "What took you so long?"

I looked at my husband. "We had to wait for a neighbor to come stay with the boys." Somehow, saying I had been waiting for him to come home from a poker game did not invoke the family image I wanted to convey.

When your water breaks, you must deliver within twenty-four hours so there is no infection. But I was not in labor. And so began the most painful process imaginable: an infusion of heavy doses of drugs to induce contractions upon a bloated body that has not entered this phase willingly. Pain meds, please!

Six intense hours later, our third boy arrived. It was the perfect ending to a series of labor days.

JUST ORDINARY MOMS

"You will understand when you're older."

GROWING TECH

My son grew up today. No, he didn't suddenly sprout a few inches or grow a beard overnight. I mean, really, this isn't a fairy tale. It is just a heart-achingly true story of coming of age in an age of technology.

When I grew up, I don't think anyone noticed. I am sure it was a realization my parents came to only when looking backward on their lives. They had me babysitting my siblings when I was only seven. There was no Red Cross certificate back then signifying that I was old enough to tend children responsibly. It just happened out of necessity because my parents both worked, and money was too tight for nannies.

At age ten, I bought my first training bra with my own money I earned from working in my father's seafood store. No one went with me to Sears for that intensely awkward and proud moment when I took my first bra to the cash register.

Nor was anyone there a couple of years later when I would purchase my first box of Tampax.

Later in high school, my best friend, who I envied because he was three years older, taught me how to drive and shuttled me to get my driver's license. He even took me to Round Table Pizza afterward to celebrate my new achievement with a pineapple and Canadian bacon pie.

In short, there were no big ceremonies and few obvious markers of my coming of age, except maybe some 8-millimeter short films of past Christmases collecting dust in the basement and a few stray, unorganized photos in boxes shoved in closets. I don't know that my parents ever had a total, whole-body experience of knowing that their daughter was no longer a child. It was all a gradual, natural progression. And I can guarantee you that if they did notice anything, technology had little or nothing to do with it.

But when my child grew up today, it was not simply looking back on a worn and faded photo that had my insides seizing and my eyes flooding with tears. It was a short series of technological moments that threw all the pieces of my known son high into the air and rearranged them anew into a completely new gestalt. Like the best kind of optical illusion, it was a "now you see him, now you don't" experience. A surge went through me like an electric shock, and I knew for sure that Josh would never quite be a child again.

It started while I was waiting in my car for Josh to finish

up his piano lesson. I heard the soft ping of my iPhone letting me know I had an e-mail message, so I quickly switched from my Kindle to my phone to see what was coming in. I cringed when I saw it was from Josh's baseball coach telling us that his Red Sox team had practice that night from 6:00 to 8:00 p.m. I remember thinking that it was good I had this cool new piece of technology, or I might have missed the communication altogether.

My husband was away yet again on another business trip, so he was not going to be able to help coach the practice and thus supervise Josh there. Josh was only ten, and we had not yet started the practice of "drop and run" for sports activities, which I yearned to do more than I liked to admit. But whenever I thought about leaving him at a sports practice, I could only think about how awful I would feel if he got hurt and I wasn't there to come immediately to his aid. So, I was not really relishing the thought of hanging out for two more hours watching the Red Sox play catch and field balls.

Once we returned home from piano, I hastily fed Josh dinner, scrambled to minimally clean up the kitchen, and prodded my son to get in the car. I felt annoyingly rushed, and more than slightly resentful, to have two precious hours just wiped from my day. It was then, in the back of my mind, that I had a niggling thought that maybe today I should just "drop and run." I thought of all the things I could get done at home, and I practically began to drool. But I quickly turned the thought away. The baseball practice was at a location brand new to both of us, an old tennis facility recently renovated into a multi-sports center. I couldn't leave him, especially when it was so unfamiliar. *Could I?*

We rushed from the house and started down the long, winding hill toward town. Although it was sunny, there was a winter chill in the air this early April day.

"Look at that beautiful tree," I said, pointing out a cherry tree that was blossoming, a veritable pink and white popcorn ball against the dull brown foliage of a late-blooming spring.

"Huh?" Josh muttered. I looked at him sitting in the back, reflected in my rearview mirror, and realized that he had not even looked up from his iPhone to behold this lovely little wonder of nature. I sighed, remembering the sweet little boy who used to chat at me incessantly from the booster in the back seat. Then that niggling thought again: He's just like a teenager—lost in his own world, separating from mine. Maybe he *is* old enough to leave at practice. After all, he does have his iPhone.

I decided in that instant to just do it. However, treating him like the little boy I still felt him to be, I went through the whole scenario with him so that he would know where I would be at every turn. I told him I was going to drop him off at the sports center and wait in the car until he found his team. Then he was to text me and let me know he was all set. At that point, I would be going home and would be back in front of the building at the end of practice.

"Are you OK with this, Josh?" I asked, half hoping he would just say no, and I would be off the hook from my daring, new self who was willing to leave her son behind.

I pulled into a parking spot directly in front of the building and watched in the rearview mirror as Josh grabbed his gear and offered a quick, "Bye, Mom," before slamming the back door.

"Don't forget to text me!" I yelled, but he was already gone, striding confidently toward the front doors of the facility.

I would like to say that I sat there calmly and waited for his text, maybe sorted through my purse, or engaged in some similarly useful task, but instead, I turned completely around in my seat and kept my eyes glued to the doors of the multi-sports center. I checked out everyone coming in or out to see if I recognized anyone from the team. Then I picked at a torn cuticle on my right hand. I was struck by how anxious I felt, even though I was still in the parking lot.

And then there was that unmistakable ping. The text "OK" lit up my screen—one small, simple word for one small, simple boy. I remember smiling and thinking, We did it! as I pulled carefully out of the parking lot and headed back home. I felt ridiculously proud of ourselves, like we had passed some important exam with an A grade.

I was barely five minutes out of the parking lot when I

heard another ping from my phone. It was a different tone, kind of a "prrriiiingg" that signals when someone has made a move against me in the scrabble-like game called Words with Friends. I quickly looked down to see who was playing. "Doodle Bubba." Josh.

Even though I do not ever play this game when I am driving, I clicked to the screen to see what word he had played in the quick five minutes we had been separated. "Tread." As a verb, it means, "to walk," as a noun, "an instant of treading, a step." My little boy is growing up, treading through his childhood and taking a step toward being an adult. And then it hit me: "Tread"—a *big* word for a *big* boy.

A knot was starting to loosen in my gut that I had not realized was even there. A soft warmth was slowly creeping through my body like a wave of bubbly bath water, and I felt tears well in my eyes. I sensed that some big realization was about to be revealed, but I was not quite grasping it yet.

And then, a different ping came from my phone, an actual ring tone—Pink Panther, to be exact. I glanced at the screen to see who was calling, not sure I wanted the moment to be broken with idle chatter. Yet, what I saw on the screen conjoined and crystallized my scattered thoughts. Josh was smiling at me from the screen. Not current Josh, but baby Josh—a pudgy, happy-go-lucky, eight-month-old smiling wide into the camera. It was the photo he had chosen to come up on the screen with his outbound calls.

"Did you get my word, Mom?"

"Yes, I did. It was a good one, too." Suddenly, I felt a momentous shift within me. I knew with an equal measure of sadness and joy that the Josh I just dropped off was not this baby looking at me now. In fact, he was not even the same Josh I had dropped off anxiously at the sports center minutes before. Josh was growing up, treading steadily to adulthood, with iPhone fully attached and functional, even essential somehow. As sad/happy tears ran down my cheeks, I headed for home as a "new" mom with a "new" grown-up son, thinking, I need to write about how Josh grew up today.

"*It looks like a bomb went off in here!*"

JUST AN ORDINARY DAY

*I*t is the first day of school. Ever! First-grader Corey watches out the window for the bus, adorably dressed in a preppy blue and white striped shirt and khaki shorts, his hair slicked back like Dad's. His backpack, full of supplies he excitedly picked out at the drugstore, is at his side. Wow, he is actually ready *and* on time for the bus!

The baby, Chris, starts to cry, so I walk around the kitchen breast-feeding him while helping three-year-old Robert get ready for nursery school. Thank goodness today is someone else's turn to carpool because it is not even 8:00 a.m., and already things seem a little hectic around here.

"Bus is here!" yells Corey, so we all walk the new schoolboy out to the bus. I smile, wave goodbye, and then turn around, take Robert's hand, and start to cry. He looks up at me with his beautiful brown eyes and says, "Don't worry,

Mommy, he be back."

We dawdle on our way back to the house when suddenly I realize that Robert will be picked up in fifteen minutes, and he has not eaten yet. He is a very slow eater and finishes only half a glass of milk and a few bites of peanut butter toast when I hear the carpool beeping. Out he goes.

Chris starts to cry again, and I get the whiff of a big nasty diaper. Changed and fed again, he is ready for a nap.

All is quiet for a minute, and I think about grabbing a cup of tea when the phone rings. It is the mom who drove the carpool this morning. "When I dropped the kids off at preschool, the teacher was looking for the snacks—I guess it was your turn today. Just thought you should know." Shoot. Too late now.

I look at the floor and remember I was going to clean it today. I usually wash the floor in the middle of the night when Chris wakes me to feed, but he has slept straight through the night for the past two weeks. This has been great, but the floor is filthy. I clean up the dishes, wash the kitchen floor, fold laundry, change the sheets, start more laundry, look through the mail, and now Chris is crying, and I wonder why he took such a short nap, although according to the clock, he's been sleeping for two hours. I sigh. My cold cup of tea is still on the counter.

As soon as I am done feeding Chris, Robert gets dropped off back home. We run around and play soccer for a while, with Chris on my back in the baby backpack, bouncing around. This is my Mommy workout. We are all starving now, so I fix a peanut butter sandwich for Robert (no judging, please—it's all he will eat). He sits down next to me as I am feeding Chris, grabs one of the stuffed animals, and shoves it under his shirt. "What are you doing?" I ask.

"I best-feeding, too!"

Maybe I should stop breast-feeding in front of a three-year-old, but then when and where am I going to do it?

Time for Chris's afternoon nap. "Chris is sleeping, so what would you like to do?" I ask Robert.

No hesitation here: "Let's make cookies!" In no time, the kitchen counters, and some of the walls, are coated in flour, eggs, and cream. Numerous chocolate chips have found their way to the floor, and more than a few are ground in from being stepped on. So much for the clean floor.

Through the kitchen window, I see Corey's bus going up the street, but no Corey in the yard. I missed his bus. It is only the first day of the school year and I can already give up all hope of any mother-of-the-year award. Will the bus driver turn around and drop him off?

I wonder what to do about the bus, but before I can figure it out, Robert is pulling on my leg. "Mommy, I had an explosion!" He was potty trained before the baby was born but reverted back after Chris arrived. Hopefully the preschool teachers will not become aware of this, as I think potty training just might be a requirement to attend school. I am not looking forward to that phone call.

I am expecting to see full-blown diarrhea coming down his leg, but when I look in the back of his pants, there is nothing. "It's OK, Robert, you must have just had some gas."

"No, Mommy! I had an *explosion!*"

"No, you didn't; there is nothing in your pants."

"Yes, yes, my peanut exploded!"

"What?" I look down inside the front of his pants, and there stands his little penis, straight and tall. I muffle a snort of laughter. "Oh, OK, Robert. Don't worry, the explosion will go away."

"But I don't like it," he says, looking a little scared.

That's what you think, I say to myself, shaking my head to keep from laughing.

A moment later, I hear the bus returning (thank you, Mr. Bus Driver!), and Corey navigates the three giant steps down. He runs to the open front door where I am waiting.

I give him a big hug, "How was school?"

"Great," he says, then drops his pack, grabs a handful of cookies, and runs upstairs. I'll let him play with his brother and catch up with his news later.

As I am beginning to make dinner, my mommy radar kicks in. Before, there were the normal sounds of laughter and thumping and crashes coming from the playroom. Now, I hear nothing. Not a good sign when two little boys are playing.

I run upstairs to investigate and see Corey standing over my closed suitcase. "Where is Robert?" I quaver, already knowing the answer.

Corey points to the suitcase, which has a combination lock. His thumb is clicking the cylindrical dials.

"Why did you put him in there?" I shriek.

"He wanted to go in." Calm yourself, I think. You know the combination. I try one number. Another. Another. No, apparently I don't know the combination.

I run downstairs to grab a knife to cut open the suitcase. I rap on the edge of the suitcase and yell, "Robert, honey, move over to this side of the suitcase. I am going to cut you out!" As I pound on the side, the numbers come back to me. Success! The suitcase pops open and Robert pops out, all smiles.

My husband, Paul, arrives just in time to sit down for dinner, and then it is bath time. Many years later, I will learn that there were no fond memories of bath time because I scoured them clean. How else are you going to get grass stains off those knees?

I wipe up the floor while Paul scoops up Chris and the boys get into their jammies. I call Corey and Robert into my room for their bedtime story. We all like to snuggle together on The Big Bed. Corey comes in, but not Robert. I holler down the stairs, "Paul, send Robert up. We are waiting for him. It's story time."

"He's not down here."

"Funny, Husband."

"No, really."

"He is not up here, either."

"Robert?"

"Robert!" No response. It is early September, still daylight, and the first place you look when a three-year-old child is missing is the pool, and then the woods. I am yelling in the back; my husband is yelling in the front. I run back inside the house. Frantically, I search and search, then go back outside and yell "Robert!" some more. For thirty minutes, we are in and out of the house, searching and yelling.

My neighbor must have heard us. "What is the matter?"

"We can't find Robert!"

"I'll help." He enters the house and methodically checks room by room. Not five minutes later, from upstairs I hear, "I found him!" Robert is fast asleep under the sink in the bathroom.

Paul and I are exhausted, having been scared out of our minds. And now we feel a little silly as well. We wake Robert, and he is ready for the bedtime story. Then it's lights out for all of us.

The next day begins with Robert bouncing on The Big Bed at 6:30 a.m., happily shouting, "It's morning time. I want to make your bed!" Why is he awake at 6:30 a.m., and why does he want to make our bed? Then I remember—last night's story was about a mother who did all the work in the house, and her husband and boys did none. She got fed up and left, and they all turned into pigs! Oh, boy—I am definitely not taking that book back to the library just yet. We will read that one again and again for several more nights, and soon they will be dusting, vacuuming, doing the laundry, cleaning bathrooms, ironing, and cooking dinner.

I pull Robert into bed between us, and he falls back to sleep. I lie there and continue my own little dream about someday not having my entire life become engulfed by ordinary tasks. But then again, I wouldn't really change a single thing.

"*If I've told you once,
I've told you a thousand times...*"

MY LEGACY OF CHOICE

I have a mother confession. Sometimes I want to walk away from my life, from my beautiful, happy-go-lucky son who is always smiling, from my husband of fifteen years who truly has lived the vow "to have and to hold, in sickness and in health," from my beautiful home that has been so lovingly remodeled to fit my tiniest of whims, and from my loyal golden retriever and the silky calico cat that will sleep only with me, curled perfectly in the cradle formed by my bent, warm legs. Sometimes I want to walk away, going nowhere in particular, except to get away from the heaviness I feel as a mother—from all the doubt, guilt, responsibility, and fear.

"This is not news," you say. "Every mother feels this way at some point in her life. It's normal. Don't be so hard on yourself."

Except that as a child, I was left, and more than once. The

first time was thirty-seven years ago.

Picture a long, lanky five-year-old kid with stringy fawn-colored hair. It is a typical northern California morning—a cloudless, light-blue sky, a soft light that doesn't call undue attention to itself, not too hot, not too cold. It is the kind of day that is boring and forgettable—unless your mother is about to leave you for good.

I am hanging upside down on my jungle gym, probably trying to make the day a little more interesting. I am starting to feel that tingle in my toes and warmth in my head that means there really is lifeblood in there, and it is starting to pool in my bored little brain. I am hanging facing the back of the house and can now see my long-limbed mother walking slowly towards me. I swing my arms out to make sure I am seen, sort of a toned-down "Look, Mom, I'm upside down!" antic, but trying to be more mature than that.

She's my idol, my mother. She is the only mom I know who teaches her daughter to eat artichokes and edamame. She speaks to me of philosophy, Jungian archetypes, and comparative religion. While I haven't a clue what she means, I nod like I do and give her my ever-eager ear. She says I am a very good girl. I am honored to know her and work so hard to be her star pupil, the light of her life. Yet there is so little light in her serious, brooding way.

Little do I know that she suffers from a severe mood disorder. I take the daily temperature of her mood like a studied meteorologist. If there is rain, I bring out the figurative umbrella. I stay quiet and out of the way or play her favorite song to her, "Greensleeves," over and over again on my Fisher Price phonograph. Lately, there has been a lot of rain, a lot of "Greensleeves." There is an increasing vacancy to her that makes me try even harder to bring her back to life.

On this boring, uneventful day, I hang upside down, craving my idol's attention. Yet, she tells me she is leaving, that she is taking everything with her and will not ever return. Her face is utterly impassive, unreadable. She looks at me for a long moment, maybe wondering if I am going to come down or make a scene, but I just hang there, arms akimbo, blood really rushing now, the part of my legs that connect with the bar beginning to ache in protest.

She turns abruptly and walks toward the side of the house. She's heading for the car. *She really means it!* I want to run after her, grab her by the arm, and beg her to stay, but I am frozen. It seems right, somehow, to remain in this position, upside down. I don't trust that if I come down, my tingly, bloodless legs will hold me. I don't trust that the ground will be solid beneath my feet. Somehow, the pressure of the bar against my knees, though painful, is the only thing that feels real— that and the horrible, sickening ache that has started in my chest and is creeping, slowly, but surely, into my belly.

***

Six years later, things had changed, at least on the surface.

My father was remarried, and I had new stepsiblings. But my father was often away on business, as he was on that critical winter evening. My stepmother had put me in charge of my three-year-old half-brother, seven-year-old sister, and eleven-year-old stepsister while she went out. She did not tell us where she was going.

I was eleven years old like my stepsister, but I acted like I was going on forty. I was anxious, a perfectionist, and ultra-responsible, so I was often left alone with my siblings, even though it completely petrified me. I was so afraid of being left at home parentless that I often chased my father's car down the block when he left, tears streaming down my face, terror seizing my every nerve. I pumped my legs as fast as I could make them go, screaming at the top of my lungs for him to stop. But he never did. I was convinced that he would leave me, too, that I wouldn't matter enough to bring him home again.

On that night, with both my parents gone and myself put in charge, I swallowed my panic like oversized pills. I was nearly choking with anxiety. I became a drill sergeant and somehow managed to get everyone dinner, variations on PB&J. But I was only partially present. My mind hummed constantly with obsessive thoughts: Where is she? Will she be back soon? Do I hear the car in the driveway? Did she say when she would be home?

We watched TV, and I watched my siblings laugh at the

sitcom. It was all I could do to just sit there. I was crawling out of my skin, completely buzzing with anticipation and worry. I also felt stabbing bolts of envy at my siblings' lightness and laughter—their childhood. I cried out inside with rage and anguish. I don't want to be the adult. I want my mommy.

I made everyone go to bed, too early I know, but sleep seemed the only antidote to this awful waiting. It took me a while to settle in my bed. I had little rituals I did to make myself feel safe, like bringing the covers all the way up to my chin to discourage a murderer from slashing my throat. I covered my chest with crossed wrists, lest a madman try to shoot me in the heart. And then I prayed—for safety, for freedom from fright, and for my mom to come home soon.

Finally, blessed sleep. A reprieve. No dreams. Peace.

I knew it was morning because I heard the birds chirping outside the window. The light was barely visible through the shades I had drawn to keep burglars from looking in. While my eyes opened and tried to focus, my thoughts immediately went to my stepmother. I thought she must be home, but I did not understand why she hadn't woken us for school. *Surely* she is home.

I woke up my stepsister, and together we crept down the hall toward my parents' bedroom, giggling with nervousness, fearful yet guardedly optimistic. I stopped halfway down the hall because the door was open. I was gagging on those oversize pills of panic again, and nausea was moving in. My sister got to the door and screamed, "She's not there, and the bed hasn't been slept in at all!"

***

Years later, I spend countless hours in a therapist's office recounting story after story similar to these. Stepmothers who put me in charge of things no child should ever have to deal with, siblings being shipped out to relatives and friends because "they are too hard to manage," and the loss of siblings and mothers to three separate divorces in a span of ten years.

On this particular day in my early forties, I am once again on my therapist's couch. It is rainy and gray outside, a more than fitting accompaniment to my dark, hopeless mood. I tearfully blurt out my terrible mother confession. "I want to walk away from my life." Shame fills my every pore so that I think my body might actually sob, too. I cannot look Meredith, my faithful therapist of ten years, in the eye. And yet, instead of criticism and horror, I receive empathy and insight in response.

"Can you see it is no wonder you feel overwhelmed and terrified as a mom? You never had a role model of a responsible and capable mother in your life," Meredith says, appealing to an empathic place buried somewhere in my mess of internal scar tissue.

"You were given way too much responsibility for a child.

But, on top of that, the responsibility was coupled with catastrophic loss and terror. Being responsible for another human being is awfully loaded for you."

I feel a momentary blanket of self-love and understanding being laid over me, but it is so terribly heavy with utter sadness for that little girl who tried so hard but was left anyway. The sadness is completely bottomless and mingles with my intense mother angst and doubt, until I do not think I can ever feel any lower or more wretched.

"I don't think it would even matter if I left," I sob. "All my son, Grant, wants is Daddy, Daddy, and Daddy. The first thing he asks in the morning is, 'Where is Daddy?' When I pick him up at the bus stop, he says, 'Why didn't Daddy come get me?' When I leave for a night out with friends, he doesn't even say goodbye. I think I want to leave because it just doesn't seem to matter that I'm even here."

Meredith smiles at me knowingly. She knew this was coming, and she is prepared. Her voice is soft, even, and comforting, flowing like warm water from my head where I first register it, through my chest, then down into my limbs.

"You absolutely do matter—you are the very core of Grant's universe. You are like air to him. He needs you every second of every day but is completely unaware of your presence. He breathes you in but doesn't see you—you are his *air*."

I am his air. The tears that have been streaming down my

face come even faster now. I know she is right, but I don't want her to be right. If she is right, then I have to face the awful truth that my mother was *my* air, and it was sucked right out of me.

"Meredith, how could I even think of leaving Grant after all I have been through? How could I even begin to entertain the possibility of hurting my son that way? When I, more than anyone, know what it is like to be left."

"First of all, all moms have thoughts like these from time to time. It is just part of being a mother—" Meredith ventures.

I am terribly impatient with this comment and rudely interrupt her. "I *know* I can't be the first to think this, but how could *I* think this?"

Meredith calmly continues. "The crucial difference between you and other mothers who have these thoughts is that, for you, the theoretical is real. One who has never been left feels a certain sense of safety when thinking about abandoning her family because it truly is just a thought, not necessarily a realistic option."

I'm beginning to get it. "You mean for them, leaving isn't a real possibility because they haven't lived it?"

"Yes," Meredith says. "When you think about leaving, you know it can really happen because it did, to you. Unfortunately for you, these thoughts will always carry the traumatic weight of your past. You can't think you want to leave without remembering that you were left and that you, too, can really leave."

***

So this is my legacy. I will forever acutely feel the pain of losing my own mother(s) at the same time that I know I can potentially walk out on my own son. It is a legacy I never thought I would own—a double-edged sword that cuts me to the quick every time I feel overwhelmed and discouraged as a mother. Because I was left, I know I can leave. This painful knowledge forces me to make a conscious choice each time I feel like abandoning my family. It is the ultimate irony in my life—that the legacy of helpless abandonment is the continual dictate of choice. And so, I choose to stay, over and over, again and again. For I am *air*, and I do matter.

"Do as I say, not as I do."

MILLION-DOLLAR MOM

From the hallway upstairs, where I had gathered another load of laundry, I heard the faint buzzing of the oven timer—a reminder that it was time to start the climb up our quarter-mile-long driveway to greet the middle-school bus carrying my fourth-grade daughter, Jillian.

I arrived at the end of the driveway just as the bus turned the corner at the bottom of our hilly street and watched it stop at the first house to make a drop-off. I gave my neighbor a quick wave as her son jumped off the bus and joined her.

The bus began its slow ascent up our street, huffing and puffing like an old man, and then pulled up beside me. The driver gave me a silent nod as the folding doors opened. I waited patiently for Jillian as she made her way through a sea of flailing body parts that were partially obstructing the narrow bus aisle. She paused on the landing, gave me a big smile, and then turned to say goodbye to the bus driver. She worked her way down the steep stairs to exit the bus, practically landing in my arms as she lurched forward from the weight of her overstuffed pink, monogrammed L. L. Bean backpack.

"Hey, honey," I said as I wrapped my arms around her, and I got a nice big hug in return. At age nine, she did not yet know how uncool it is to hug your mom in public.

"Mom, wait 'til I show you what I made in art today!" she replied, dancing around as I stopped to gather the mail from the mailbox.

"Can't wait!" I said, truly meaning it.

As we walked back toward the house, I leafed through the stack of mail to see if there was anything worth opening. Among the catalogs, credit card offers, and bills, I spotted a larger envelope with bold print across the back: **Publishers Clearing House Sweepstakes: Open Immediately**. I chuckled as I imagined Ed McMahon showing up at our house to present us with that $1,000,000 check.

"What's that, Mom?"

"It's a kind of lottery, except you don't pay to do it. Your household gets assigned a number, and you can win a lot of money if that number is picked," I explained.

"Can we open it right now?" she asked.

"We'll take a look when we get in the house. While we have some chocolate chip cookies and milk," I said.

Another smile flashed my way, giving me that glowing feeling I'd had since we began this routine at the start of the school year three weeks earlier. I was still relishing the novelty of getting my children on and off the bus each day and sitting with them for an afternoon snack as they regaled me with the highlights of their day at school.

It had been only a few months since I traded in my business suit and executive's briefcase for a temporary stint as a stay-at-home mom. I was buying myself time, precious time I needed to gain perspective as I struggled to balance the fickle allure of career success with the primal desire to be with my children.

After two months of enjoying my first carefree summer at home without a job since I was in grade school, my nine-year-old, six-year-old, and I were now adjusting to a more regimented school schedule. I missed their camaraderie while they were gone during the day and eagerly awaited my time with them in the afternoon. The routines that I knew I would take for granted if I had been home full-time for the past nine years felt new and special to me right now, like a gift. I took note of these things, sensing their fleeting nature.

We stepped inside the house, and Jillian took a deep inhale. "Yum, it smells like a bakery in here," she said, spotting the still-warm cookies sitting on the kitchen table. She dumped her backpack on the landing in the hallway at the front of the house, headed for the table, and plucked a cookie off the plate, licking the bits of smeared chocolate off her fingers. "Yum, um, um," she mumbled, lost in cookie heaven.

I placed the stack of mail on the kitchen counter and joined her at the table with the Publishers Clearing House envelope in hand.

"Do you think we won, Mom?" she asked between bites of cookie and slurps of milk.

"Doubtful," I replied. "But it's still fun to think about the possibility." I ripped open the envelope and pulled out its contents. There were several pieces of paper and a sheet of stickers with our assigned number on them.

Jillian reached for one of the letters. "Look, Mom, I think we won!" she exclaimed. She handed me one of the letters, and I saw the bold writing stamped diagonally across the page. "You are a winner. Claim your prize today," it read. I was skeptical, but was now curious enough to want to read the fine print. Jillian stood up and read over my shoulder as I perused the papers. There was a lot to read, and each page referred us to some other set of instructions as if we were on a scavenger hunt.

As I scanned the fourth enclosure, still unsure of what, if anything, we had actually won, I could not help but fantasize about what a large chunk of found money would mean for us. Would I quit my job for good and stay home? I had never felt that my work was all about the money, and yet, if....

Suddenly, I felt a surge of panic that propelled me back to reality. I glanced at the clock. In all our excitement, I had forgotten to set the oven alarm a second time to remind me to head out to meet the elementary school bus. It was already 3:40, and I was not sure I was going to make it to the end of the driveway in time. Without thinking, I dashed out of the house.

It was now raining, and I realized halfway up the driveway that I was barefoot. I sprinted to the top of the driveway and watched the big yellow machine cruise past our house on the other side of the street. I got to the mailbox just in time to watch it turn the corner out of our neighborhood. "Damn it!" I exclaimed, safely out of earshot of any little people. My sides hurt from the short sprint. I bent over to catch my breath and then raced back down to our house, unsure what to do next.

My heart was pounding, my drenched hair was dripping into my eyes, and I felt nauseated and dizzy from the physical exertion. I stumbled into the house, leaving muddy puddles behind me as I entered the kitchen. I pulled out the school handbook, hands shaking, and flipped through the pages until I found the number for the school administrator's office.

"I just missed my first-grader's bus," I explained sheepishly to the woman who answered the phone. "What happens now?"

"The bus driver will bring him back to school once he

finishes his run," she said in a flat tone. I almost wondered if I had reached a recording, put on just for the likes of me. "You can pick him up here in about a half hour." She asked my name, and I was tempted to hang up before identifying myself as the inept mom who could not do something as basic as meet her child at the bus stop on time. Miss Hot Shot Professional living the Fantasy Mom dream by baking chocolate chip cookies. I mumbled my name and Danny's, put the phone down, and tried my darnedest to think clearly over the pounding of my heart.

"Jill, we've gotta run. Please get into the car," I called as I raced around the house looking for my shoes and purse. No time to change out of my wet clothes.

We drove out of our neighborhood, and I had to remind myself to pay attention to the road as I berated myself repeatedly for being such a space cadet. About four blocks from our street, I spotted the bus on a side street and pulled in to head it off at the pass. As the bus approached, I stepped out of the car and waved my arms frantically at the driver.

The bus came to a slow, squeaky halt as the stop sign unfurled from its side arm and the flashing lights turned on. Jillian got out of the car and joined me as we stood outside the bus, waiting. As the doors folded open, my son emerged at the top of the stairs, a little body inside a large yellow rubber slicker with a duckbill visor framing his baby face. He stepped tentatively down the stairs, and I saw that his cheeks were stained with tears.

"You forgot about me, Mom," he said in a tiny voice, reminding me again of how I had let him down. I reached out to scoop him up off the last step of the bus, to prove my love for him, but he hopped off to my left, past my outstretched arms, which sheepishly made their way back down to my sides, embarrassed by the false start.

"But, Danny, we might have won a million dollars," Jillian said cheerfully, certain that this news more than compensated for my little infraction.

"We'll just have to pay half of it to the government in taxes anyway," my six-year-old replied as he opened the car door and flopped down on the back seat.

Under different circumstances, I might have laughed with delight at this surprising quip from my precocious first-grader. I would have swelled with pride at how bright he was, clearly a reflection of fine parenting. Instead, I slinked into the driver's seat, took a quick peek in the rearview mirror to make sure everyone was safely buckled in, and headed for home, freshly humbled by the subtle challenges of full-time motherhood.

"Stop that, or you'll be grounded for life!"

CLICK

A dark cloud of fury filled the car as he packed himself in, an awkward kinetic sculpture of gangly, teenage limbs harnessed by an oversized backpack. He stared straight ahead with an angry scowl, a visible broadcast that he hated me with all of his being, more than any teenager had ever hated a parent before. I was the most reviled parent on the planet; he made that clear.

His loathing nurtured the perpetual state of anxiety that had taken up residence in my gut ever since our parent/teenager relationship had deteriorated over the past year. Or was it on the day he had turned seventeen? Either way, whenever life placed us in proximity, whether in person or in my dreams, dread and unease twisted in my stomach, forcing sour bile swirling upward, even when I had not eaten for hours. That sickening feeling had become so commonplace that I was almost able to ignore it. Or maybe one of these times I would actually vomit—what would he think of that?

I intentionally turned to the left so he wouldn't think I was trying to look at him, twisting to see behind the car so I could safely slide out of the parking spot. Giving him space, as they say.

"How was school today?" I asked, at the same time chiding myself for repeating the same inane question every single freakin' day. Why couldn't I be more creative? Why couldn't I engage this child? We had turned into caricatures—an overbearing mother (am I?) and an angry, troubled teenager (is he?).

"I made chicken parm for supper," I ventured. Yet another one of my useless attempts to connect with him. Chicken parmigiana with savory sauce over linguine was definitely one of his favorite meals—couldn't I tempt him just a little?

He stared straight ahead, unblinking, in an unresponsive teenage coma, seething on the inside and dead on the outside. I turned up the radio louder and bounced my head a little with the music to show that I was unmoved by his attempts to break me, happy in *my* life, diggin' the classic rock station that we both liked. Mid-song during "Ramblin' Man" by the Allman Brothers, he punched the buttons until he found a grungy voice singing in monotone, one of the new releases from a current band. I recognized this song, too, and began to move my head in slow, low grooves to show that we had this music in common as well.

He proved me wrong. "That song sucks," he said as he attacked the radio buttons again.

Every day I drove our son home from school in this fashion. It was the fall of his senior year of high school, a time that he should be out having fun with his friends, flirting with the bevy of identically honey-haired and impossibly gorgeous girls who hang out at Starbucks or drag racing neighboring kids up our country lane. But our boy had lost his driving privileges three weeks into the school year due to a toxic combination of lying, hints of disreputable activities, and his unacceptable, ungrateful, unhelpful, unhealthy, un-everything attitude at home. His anger stemmed from his opinion that none of this behavior should matter; he should be able to do as he pleased. Not having rights to the car and being driven to and from school by his parents was unfair and abysmal, and he hated us for it.

Yet our love for him was so powerful, it literally hurt. Sometimes my husband and I lay awake at night staring at the ceiling in silent, independent agony, each knowing the other was suffering but unable to help one another because of our own individual bewilderment. I hoped we would someday recover from the torture of this love.

The boy was due to get his car back in another week or so

if he shaped up even just a little bit, but so far things were not looking good. I presumed he planned to try to rally on the very last day, at the very last minute, just like he did for everything else, including completing his school assignments at 4:00 a.m. on the due date. It drove me crazy that seemingly no matter what time during the night I awoke from whatever restless sleep I occasionally managed to steal, a faint glow from the light in his room escaped from under his door and dimly lit the hallway, broadcasting his dysfunctional study habits.

An A student during his freshman and sophomore years, he was just barely pulling C's now. How this kid was expected to get into and succeed in college, we had no idea. But my husband and I desperately needed him to get into a college, *any* college, and to *go*! Instead of looming lonely, the hopeful dream of a peaceful empty nest called out to us like a soothing siren just beyond the horizon of our daily reality. We simply needed a break.

The rural lane heading home travels through a natural wildlife preserve. Narrow, shoulderless pavement is closely lined on both sides with huge trees that stand like rows of silent sentinels. It is a lovely drive that consumes most of the distance from the school to our neighborhood.

In the midst of this scenic and familiar route, the roaring sound of air rushing in the passenger window suddenly overwhelmed the music from the radio as the boy unclicked his seatbelt and popped himself up and halfway out of the downed window. He rested himself on the edge of the opening with his upper body completely up and out of the car, his gray T-shirt whipping in the wind.

Get down! What on earth are you doing? What the hell is wrong with you, anyway? I did not say any of those things.

Cautiously, I braked to slow the car, but there was no room at the road's edge to pull over, so we went along like that for some distance. I nervously pictured an over-reaching tree branch knocking him under the wheels. Finally he slid back down into his seat and rebuckled his seatbelt.

I tried to keep it light. "What are you, a dog?"

"I've always wanted to do that," he replied. "It felt good." He unbuckled again. I slowed down some more. He buckled. I sped back up. He unbuckled. I braked again.

"Sorry, but the law in this state says everyone must wear their seatbelts. Please stop doing that," I bade.

He buckled. I sped back up. He unbuckled. Buckled. Unbuckled. Buckled. Unbuckled. Click click click click click.

We arrived at an intersection with a stop sign, so I could halt the car without fear of someone zooming around a curve and rear-ending us. I looked at him, no doubt with "that look" on my face. "Please stop."

Click click click. Then he sat still, buckled. I kept my eyes on him a moment more, then turned back to face the road again. As I moved the car into the intersection, I heard click

click click and then and there completely lost my cool. I floored the gas pedal, flew across the intersection to a dirt area where people park to take hikes, stomped on the brakes, thrust the gearshift into park, and glared at my darling boy with a look that definitely did not say "darling." Without a word, he got out of the car and began to walk up the road ahead.

I watched the distance between us grow, then shifted into drive and eased alongside him. "Are you walking home?" I asked through the open window. No response, not even a glance. So I drove away. Just drove away. Up the winding, hilly road, drowning in a flood of conflicted feelings. I felt guilty. I felt justified. I felt furious yet almost found myself laughing at the ridiculousness of this argument, if that was what you could even call it. I contemplated circling back and at the same time calculated how long it would take him to walk the few miles home. I was astonished at how such tiny events had escalated so quickly into such a huge chasm, and yet I realized this moment had been brewing for a long time. Mostly, I just felt horrible as I faced the truth: I had literally abandoned my child.

Back at home, I bustled around the household trying not to picture him trudging along. Of course, he had started up the wrong side of the road, and if I dared to imagine a car careening up from behind.... "Stop it!" I forcibly told myself. But after a half an hour or so, I dialed his cell phone. If he was at all civil, I would go pick him up.

I heard his phone ringing nearby—in the back part of the house! He's here? When? How?

I followed the sound to the mudroom where disappointment flushed through me all the way down to my toes. The ringing was coming from his backpack that I had brought in from the car. He didn't have his phone; I did.

As I baked up the chicken parm, I hoped it might draw him in somehow. Could I redirect the wind to waft the rich aroma in his direction? Blow extra love his way to help ease his teenage pain?

When my husband came home from work a couple of hours later, I managed to blurt out, "I left Tommy by the side of the road three hours ago, and he hasn't made it home yet," before I burst into tears.

A friend I had invited to join us for dinner showed up, and I went over the day's events with her in exhaustive detail. She's a close friend who never had children but who often lent a sympathetic ear to our teenage-raising horror stories over the past several years.

Actually, it was only during the last few months that the stories had become ominous. Our older boy had passed through high school with just a little beer drinking and pot smoking while continuing to get good grades. This younger one scared us. His need to be the social center of attention created a strong pull on him to provide "entertainment" for his friends. We were constantly on edge, imagining how far he might take it. Daily phone calls from the dean's office at school were not helping the situation. This kid could get in trouble for anything, including making the girls laugh in choir. Could he truly accumulate enough bad behavior reports to get himself kicked out? Or perhaps more likely, commit some enormous, glorious, crash-and-burn offense that would bring him great fame among his peers, followed by instant expulsion by the faculty?

It was getting dark outside and a bit chilly, which I was secretly glad about since I hoped the cold would encourage him to come home to get warm. Where *was* he? Surely he would walk in the door any second.

With artificial gaiety, my husband, our dinner guest, and I sat down at the table with one empty chair, and made meaningless conversation while munching on salad with pears and blue cheese, crisp green beans, and the chicken parm, which now stuck on the lump growing ever larger in my throat—a tumor of regret that choked me with every bite. For dessert I served a velvety lemon cake drizzled with vanilla glaze, also made especially for the boy. The boy who had been abandoned by his mother and who consequently was not at home for his favorite dinner.

We live in the middle of nowhere, surrounded by hundreds of acres of dedicated open space with an occasional housing development threaded through. I thought of possible friends' houses along the way where he might have gone, but none came to mind between the dirt patch where I had left him and our home. Besides, what would I say when I called? "Hello, this is Tommy's mom. Is he by any chance there? See, I left him by the side of the road and—never mind. Thanks anyway. Goodbye."

I thought of driving around with flashlights, but the woods are so vast we'd need a helicopter with searchlights to do any good. I thought of reporting a missing person, but he wasn't really *missing*, was he? More than once, I thought of the morgue.

I stood at the picture window peering out into the dark woods and gestured "come in" in case he was out there amid the endless trees, watching us. Eventually our friend left and the evening hours passed as my husband and I pretended to watch TV. He finally went to bed. I left the TV on and curled up under a blanket on the loveseat, knowing that if I got into bed, I would simply stare at the ceiling in the dark. Our dreams of an empty nest had unexpectedly come true, and it was a nightmare.

Just after one in the morning the back door opened, and the tall, lanky shadow that was our son came in. Relief and anger swirled together, making foul soup in my belly. I heard myself screaming, "Where were you? We were so worried! Why did you do this? I'm so happy to see you!"

"Hi," was what I actually said. "There's leftover chicken

parm if you're hungry." He started to fix himself a plate of food, so I simply added, "Good night. I'll see you in the morning," like nothing out of the ordinary had occurred.

"'Night," he echoed back, sounding unexpectedly normal.

I climbed the stairs reflecting on how the afternoon had played out. With each step, the agonizing truth became more and more clear. The dreadful heaviness I felt was not merely guilt and self-punishment because I was a terrible mother who had abandoned her child. No, the gaping, raw reality finally clicked: *He* had undeniably abandoned *me*.

"What's meant to be is meant to be."

CAUGHT UNAWARE

I almost died while giving birth to my second child. We were all caught unaware: my husband and I, our firstborn, the doctors, and most especially, the second son who blissfully remains unaware. Then, I spent several years fearful he would be taken from us before he reached his eighteenth birthday. He is my changeling; he is a puzzle; he is my heart.

When I found out I was expecting my second child, I admit I went through a period of guilt-ridden depression. My husband and I had a wonderful life with our "sun, moon, and stars" firstborn. He was the cutest little boy either of us had ever seen. Everywhere we went, people would stop us to comment on how adorable he was. This wonderful child would smile and coo at everyone he saw, and then when he began to talk, he would say "Hi" to all he met. He had not encountered anyone, at that point, who was not kind to him.

We lived in a lovely little bubble—Mommy teaching three days a week and Daddy racing home every day to be with his boy. We rarely went out, content to sit together on our couch, renting videos and taking turns holding, tickling, and being utterly fascinated with this amazing being we had created. Some family members shook their heads and quietly, but still audible to our ears, commented about our "needing to get a life" or "they're spoiling the kid rotten." Our friends, most of whom were still single, would stop by our cozy little Cape-style home to get a "baby fix" before heading out to downtown clubs on the weekends.

Occasionally we did grab a quick night out, with family members blessedly babysitting for us. They made fun of my instructions in a good-natured way. I look back on a piece of paper on which I had drawn the exact size a slice of hot dog had to be cut into sixths and laugh now at how my then-dating sister and future brother-in-law held up each piece of hot dog to see if it was small enough. Crazy, I know.

My oldest son turned two right in the thick of my terrible morning, afternoon, and evening sickness. The poor child had no idea why I kept rushing into the bathroom, and he would cry outside the locked door because he did not understand what was wrong with me. I was so very tired, and I became short with him. I was riddled with so much guilt—guilt for resenting his stubborn refusal to nap in the afternoons when I needed to sleep; guilt that I was so sick I could not grocery shop, let alone eat. So began his lifelong love affair with Mickey D's because it was so much easier getting him a Happy Meal than sitting at the table forcing him to eat green vegetables. I made him go to the "time out" chair so often because he acted out. I saw him turn more and more to his father for companionship and comfort.

For me, it was like watching a movie, hating the mother in it and hating myself even more for being that mother. I did not want to deal with an Energizer bunny of a toddler. I secretly resented the growing baby in my womb for making me feel ill and tired, too tired to do anything more than the basics with our beloved sun, moon, and stars. Then one day, I got a much-needed wake-up call.

Coming home from a friend's grad school graduation party, I started cramping. I was so afraid. I rushed to the bathroom and saw some blood—not a lot, but enough to scare me. I rummaged through the linen closet for a pad. My husband lifted me into our bed, trying to be brave and helpful, and yet the look of powerlessness on his face broke my heart. He wanted this baby and was afraid for me at the same time.

Despite my protests not to bother anyone, he called our neighbor, who had two teenage children of her own and a calm presence that I valued and had enjoyed from the moment I met her. She came right over, made me a cup of tea, placed pillows behind my back, and let me cry and carry on, letting all of my poisonous guilt flow out of me, the toxicity replaced by the knowledge and certainty that I wanted this baby. She calmly told me that sometimes these things happen for a reason, and if God meant for this baby to be born, he would be, and if it wasn't meant to be at this time, then there's a reason for that as well. She told me that I needed to sleep, to rest as often as I could, and to enjoy my time with the firstborn because, "These golden days with just one child will never happen again." And she quite forcefully told me to stop beating myself up. "All mothers feel resentment, and the best mothers feel guilt, for we never think what we do for our children is ever good enough."

The bleeding stopped somewhere in the night, and I went to my OB/GYN group the next morning. Back then, normally healthy twenty-somethings did not have ultrasounds, and fetal heartbeat detectors were not as powerful as they are today. So at eleven weeks along, I was told it was too early to hear a heartbeat, to go home and rest, and that if I continued to bleed, "Mother Nature will take care of it." They told me to come back in a week unless I developed a fever or serious abdominal pain, in which case I should go to a hospital right away. I was scared but oddly secure that I had not lost the baby. Sure enough, a week later, I was still pregnant.

The morning sickness subsided into occasional bouts of nausea, and my mood greatly improved. My two-year-old was fascinated by my growing belly and loved to talk and sing to "my little baby in Mommy's tummy."

The pregnancy continued normally. I did have vivid, crazy dreams with this pregnancy, such as this one: he was a test-tube baby and I could see him so clearly growing in a giant glass tube. I saw that he was a boy and knew that although I wanted a daughter, I was happy that my firstborn would have a brother to play with. In one dream, I was married to a man who was the complete opposite of my real husband. I remember loving him very much, while also feeling our union was frowned upon, as it seemed to take place in a more restrictive society than we live in now. This man's mother even yelled at me for getting pregnant. She said we were not right for each other, that the baby would have an awful life, and that I should just give it up for adoption. In spite of it all, we lived happily in the attic of a big, old house and I can still see that, despite the shabby furniture, we tried to make it pretty.

One dream in particular bothered me for more than a decade and a half after my child was born. The dream was so real, my heart pounded, and I was shaking for what seemed like hours after I woke. In the dream, I was visited by aliens who told me they had given me this child to take care of, and they would be back for him when he was sixteen years old. The only person I told about this dream was my husband. Thus, when this child became fascinated from an early age with his wide network of imaginary friends; his love of science fiction; his almost obsessive fascination with space travel, aliens, ghosts, and anything else deemed paranormal, we secretly feared the dream would come true. On his sixteenth birthday, I prayed that he would not be taken from us. I spent half the year in fear and the other half chiding myself for being so silly. When he turned seventeen, I was so relieved. I told him about my dream and my unreasonable fears. He laughed and said, "That would've been cool, because then we would know that aliens existed." He has a knack for turning a stressful situation or uncomfortable topic into something funny, and he always finds a way to make me laugh.

My water broke on a cold, clear, sunny, January day. I went to my doctor to confirm this fact, as the fluid did not come out in a sudden explosive gush like it does on TV but trickled oddly out of me only if I stood. The evening before, as I lay in bed, I had heard my bones grinding—the ischial spine in my pelvis opening in anticipation of the upcoming birth. It was one of the oddest sounds I have ever heard, sort of like grinding teeth, but not exactly. I was a little afraid, alternately letting my imagination get the best of me while thinking of all the alien movies I had seen where a hideous creature claws its way out of a woman's womb, yet knowing deep in my heart that this was going to be a perfectly healthy, human baby.

I was admitted to the hospital and waited for hours as my labor slowed to nothing. Whispered consultations were conducted in the corner of my hospital room. A male doctor, not my own, burst into the room demanding to know who administered the "fern test" that was supposedly positive, confirming rupture of the embryonic sac. More tests were done, and, yes, the fluid was amniotic.

A kind male resident doctor came into my room and explained how he was going to break my water. (This was his first time, and I sensed how nervous he was.) I was understandably confused—wasn't I leaking already? He explained that I probably had a tear higher up on my placenta that had caused some fluid to drip. The explanation seemed logical, and as he sat on my hospital bed, fear clearly visible on his face, he did what he had to do. He continued to sit on my bed as a waterfall of amniotic fluid coursed over his lap and onto the floor. It sounded like a roaring ocean to my ears, and we just sat there staring at each other in amazement. Then I began to laugh, and apologized to him. He laughed, too, and our room suddenly filled with nurses who all began applauding and congratulating him because all good OB/GYN docs need to be "christened" in their residency by doing just what he did—sitting on the bed with the patient, being caught unaware, and getting drenched. Apparently, they don't prepare the docs-in-training for this in med school.

I was given Pitocin to help speed up the labor. I almost

died twice. My blood pressure dropped to nothing, and I started to leave this world. I felt as if I were falling down a rabbit hole and then shooting upward as if I had wings. I jerked back and forth and upside down. So many images flew like debris swirling in a tornado funnel. I believe I saw different lifetimes as I frantically tried to hold on to something to keep me grounded. My last vision was being aware of drowning in a dark, murky pond. As I looked up, I could see a watery, hazy light obscured by a thick layer of yellow autumn leaves. I began clawing my way toward the light and physically felt myself slamming so hard against my prone body that I actually sat straight up to faces gathered around me saying, "She's back." The anesthesiologist said, "Wow, you scared the shit out of me! I'm keeping the epi in my pocket."

A short while later, I felt the same feeling of checking out and began to whimper, "It's happening again," and was given more Epinephrine. Fortunately, we all settled down after that, and things progressed as they do. Unfortunately, I learned that the anesthesiologist died a year or so later; he liked to sample what he was giving to his patients, and he died of an overdose. He knew better and yet he, too, was caught unaware.

Finally, this child was born. He was the homeliest baby I had ever seen. He was covered with dark hair, and both ears folded down. On the top of his ears, you could see imprints of where his fingers must have curled around them so much that they actually folded in half.

When they handed him to me, he opened his eyes and stared so intently into mine that I knew he had been here before. A nurse commented, "Would you look at that baby staring at his mama? I've never seen anything like it before." I held him closer, and then he let out a big sigh, which sounded like a sigh of relief at seeing home after a long journey. He wriggled and snuggled onto my breast and fell asleep for the next twelve hours.

As everyone in the room went about their business, I noticed another little consultation going on after I delivered the placenta. Several people were examining it and whispering. I tried to prop myself up, as I was being stitched closed, to hear what they were saying. I asked a nurse what was going on, and she said they found the cause of why I was leaking amniotic fluid: There was an empty sac in the placenta. What did that mean? No one said anything, but then it occurred to me. "Was there a twin at one time?"

The nurse said, "Does it really matter?"

To this day, though, it still does matter. I had two at one time, and now I have only one. But, even though I mourn that loss, this one with the larger-than-life personality of at least two people continues to give me the gift of being "caught unaware."

"If everyone else jumped off a cliff, would you do it, too?"

LOSING MY VIRGINITY

The shiny silver flip phone smacked the bathroom floor hard and clattered across the cold, brittle tiles.

"Shit!" I said loudly and then clamped a hand over my mouth. As if my daughter, Ali, would even flinch. I had heard much worse foul language from the mouths of her friends when they did not know I was in earshot. But I did not want to wake her.

I was in the bathroom across the hall from her bedroom, grabbing clothes to fill a load of wash. Her phone had tumbled out of a side pocket of the ratty plaid lounge pants she had worn around the house yesterday and then left on the floor by the shower, right next to the clothes hamper. What does she think the hamper is for? I wondered.

For some reason, Ali had stayed home last night, unusual for a Saturday. Maybe she wasn't feeling well. I hoped she was not coming down with something, because the workload in high school was getting quite demanding and college applications were right around the corner.

I held my breath as I picked up the phone, hoping the tiny screen on the front was not shattered. Displayed on the unbroken glass I saw this:

Sun   **r u ok?**   **Pennie**
10:22am

Obviously, a text message from her best friend, Pennie Danielson. They had known each other for ten years, since first grade.

The phone felt good in my hand. It was exactly the right size and sleek shape for cupping, with just enough heft. As I held it, the warmth from my hand transferred to its center, as if it were responding to my touch. I ran my thumb along the lower ridge, and it almost leapt from my palm as it doubled in size. It was open now, inviting further exploration. I felt powerful inklings of excitement as the phone exposed its secret territory. It was so very tempting.

This was not the first time I had violated Ali's privacy by examining her cell phone. She had been caught drinking a few months before and had lost cell phone privileges, at which point I had reviewed all her text messages and found out who had supplied the alcohol and where it had been consumed. This time, though, I had no reason to snoop. Reluctantly, I gently placed the enticing Motorola on the counter.

It protested! Bzzzzzzzzzzzt, the phone purred. Touch me, touch me. I picked it up again, and like something alive, it vibrated with pleasure in my hand. A new message was on the screen.

Sun 11:37am	i hope u din do nuthin crazy hes not worth it	Pennie

Alarm flooded my consciousness.

"r u ok" and "i hope u din do nuthin crazy." What or who could possibly be threatening my sweet girl into doing something crazy? Even though I knew that further exploration might take me on a journey from which I could never return, I began to probe the private areas of the phone. The RECD button glowed with a little blue light, so I chose it first. SENT would have to wait to be satisfied.

Each message showed the time, the message, and who it was from. They went in the reverse order of time, from most recent to oldest.

Sun 2:42am	ur kiddn right?	Pennie

Sat 9:34pm	its nbd practicaly evry1 else already did it 2	Pennie

Sat 9:30pm	whr r u why u not at KCs?	Pennie

I read on to find out why she had not gone out last night.

Sat 5:55pm	i only tole sam	JD
Sat 5:54pm	hey back off	JD
Sat 5:54pm	ha ha yea u do	JD
Sat 5:53pm	why u mk such big deal	JD

Who was J. D.? I guessed it was a boy, and I tried to picture him. Had Ali mentioned him or pointed him out at a soccer game? I could not remember. She did not share much about boys with me anymore. What did he think she was making a big deal about?

Sat 4:20pm	yes please f me	Dan
Sat 4:19pm	do me 2nite i will show u how ha ha	Dan
Sat 4:18pm	no rly whats prob so wht if ur bad	Dan
Sat 4:17pm	ha ha ha ha ha ha ha ur makin me laf	Dan
Sat 4:17	ha ha ha	Dan

Sat 4:15pm	chicks think JD studly so whats prob? bitches will be jealous of your conquests haha	Dan
Sat 4:07pm	whos the boy?	Dan
Sat 4:05pm	bf prob	Dan
Sat 4:04pm	chick fight?	Dan
Sat 4:03pm	what hpn?	Dan
Sat 4:02pm	wtf?	Dan
Sat 4:00pm	hey girl whassup?	Dan
Sat 3:14pm	hear u holy roller now haha cu 2nite	KC
Sat 2:38pm	hey nice going txt me	Mari

So, Ali had an interest in the boy J. D. And who was this crude boy Dan nosing into Ali's business? And what's a holy roller in text language? I wished I knew. And K. C.'s was the party she had skipped Saturday night, right? Now, there were several texts from Pennie from Saturday afternoon.

Sat 12:45pm	later	Pennie
Sat 12:40pm	dun u like him?	Pennie
Sat 12:39pm	just do it agin he be happy ;-)	Pennie
Sat 12:38pm	get ovr it	Pennie
Sat 12:36pm	whassa mtr boy trbl?	Pennie

The next time stamp took me back into the wee hours of the night, when nothing good happens when it comes to teenagers.

Sat 3:10am	ali? Talk to me!	Pennie
Sat 3:03am	r u thr?	Pennie
Sat 2:58am	u gotta finish what u start	JD
Sat 2:57am	so wha? U kno u suck at bj that's why I fk u	JD
Sat 2:55am	don be bitch	JD
Sat 2:54am	Nuthin	JD

Why did J. D. sound so mean and angry? And what on earth had happened? Was this literal or just text talk? I had heard of sexting—was this part of their banter?

Sat 2:50am	sam told me jd making evry1 laugh	Pennie
Sat 2:49am	ur not gunna like this sam says jd says ur wr terribl	Pennie
Sat 2:34am	im at marks and the guys r talking bout u	Sara
Sat 2:28am	ali u gotta call me right now	Sara

So J. D. had talked about Ali to his friends? Where was his sense of decency? I continued to work my way backward in time.

Sat 2:09am	it feels rly good if u get used to it	Pennie
Sat 2:09am	u did it? who with?	Pennie
Sat 2:09am	last smr some guy	Pennie
Sat 2:08am	i did it in a boat wasnt easy	Pennie
Sat 2:08am	umm	Pennie

Sat 2:08am	ummmmm	Pennie
Sat 2:07am	u think?	Pennie
Sat 2:07am	is that all?	Pennie
Sat 2:07am	haha got me there	Pennie
Sat 2:06am	ur a slut now u kno	Pennie
Sat 2:06am	;-0	Pennie

My concern for what had happened to Ali grew. But Pennie seemed almost playful. Perhaps this wasn't serious; just girl talk in this day and age?

Sat 2:05am	Well sum things r private u kno	Pennie

Apparently not so private among this group of so-called friends. I dove ever deeper.

Sat 2:05am	Sam and mark 2	Pennie
Sat 2:04am	many times	Pennie
Sat 2:04am	oh bj nbd	Pennie

Sam 2:03am	tell me!	Pennie
Sat 2:03am	did u touch it?	Pennie
Sat 2:02am	so how did it happn?	Pennie
Sam 2:02am	omg	Pennie
Sat 2:01am	his rents wr out?	Pennie
Sat 2:01am	I kno!!! Tell me everything	Pennie
Sat 2:00am	I was watching tv	Pennie
Sat 1:58am	u told sam already 2	Pennie
Sat 1:58am	with sam of course he wants it all the time now	Pennie
Sat 1:57am	you little slut!	Pennie

My heart sank as I realized that *something* had definitely happened involving Ali and one of these boys, probably J. D. And next, there was a flurry of messages from him. I continued to read, going back in time....

Sat 1:54am	tired. game 2mrw	JD
Sat 1:52am	id rly just like to snuggle u right now	JD
Sat 1:52am	YES	JD
Sat 1:52am	kiss u whr ur sore	
Sat 1:52am	if I was with u id kiss u and make it bettr	JD
Sat 1:51	theres more whr that came from u kno	JD
Sat 1:50am	ur soft and warm	JD
Sat 1:48am	haven't seen many?	JD
Sat 1:46am	sry	JD

Was this tender boy the same one who would be so cruel less than two hours later? I still was not sure what had happened, but a tear fell off my face onto the keypad as I continued to press the phone's RECD button to retrieve the messages.

| Sat 1:46am | what news? | Pennie |

Sat 1:45am	Yes u wr	JD
Sat 1:43am	u wr noisey girl	JD
Sat 1:42am	Duh	JD
Sat 1:41am	i kno whr id like to be	JD
Sat 1:37am	im awake r u?	JD
Sat 1:32am	i wud make you scream	Sam
Sat 1:31am	is that a yes or no?	Sam
Sat 1:31am	did he make u wet?	Sam
Sat 1:30am	well congratulations did u like it?	Sam
Sat 1:29am	ohhhh like u did him?	Sam
Sat 1:28am	and?	Sam
Sat 1:27am	ok what is it	Sam
Sat 1:27am	u can trust me	Sam

Sat 1:26am	yes u can tell me	Sam

Sat 1:25am	home asleep is my guess whassup	Sam

Sat 1:24am	no shes not here	Sam

The intimacy of these texted snippets shocked me. And who was this Sam who would converse with Ali so boldly? Where was the romance in these raw invitations?

"r u ok?" came up next and then "i hope u din do nuthin crazy hes not worth it." I had completed the received message cycle.

"i hope u din do nothing crazy hes not worth it." Wasn't that the truth! These were all awful boys as far as I could tell. I decided Pennie was a good friend, if perhaps a bad influence. Of course, it seemed that Ali had made Friday evening's decisions all on her own.

I only had one side of the story, and already my heart was breaking. And now it was time to hear the voice of my daughter. I pressed the SENT button. This time the name showed who Ali's messages had been sent to. Again they went from most recent backward into the past.

Sun 3:24am	I have to move away or jump off a fucking bridge	Pennie

Shit! No wonder Pennie had asked if Ali was OK. Was Ali

even in her room? In three huge leaps, I reached her bedroom door and turned the knob.

The lump under the covers told me she was in the bed, and the subtle movement up and down told me the lump was alive.

My body sagged against the hallway wall, and I let out a deep sigh of relief before I continued my assault on the phone. My touch was no longer gentle and I no longer cared if the damn thing broke. I jabbed at the SENT button hard, again and again, reading swiftly as Ali's messages to others tracked from recent to older once again.

Sat 9:42pm	no one at school will ever look at me the same they all kno	Pennie
Sat 9:37pm	I hate him	Pennie
Sat 9:36pm	I don care i feel like shit	Pennie
Sat 9:32pm	cant face evryn	Pennie

No wonder she had not gone out last night. Her so-called friends were talking about her, and she was embarrassed.

| Sat 5:56pm | well sam told evryn else | JD |

Sat 5:55pm	how wud u feel?	JD
Sat 5:54pm	not funny fu jerk	JD
Sat 5:54pm	u tell evry1 i suck	JD
Sat 5:53pm	why u telling evry1 bout me?	JD
Sat 4:25pm	U asshole plz stop talking bout me	JD

I noticed over an hour had passed before J. D. had replied to her on Saturday afternoon. How awful that must have been for her, alone, waiting, knowing he was out there exercising his full bragging rights over whatever they had done.

Why do kids reveal each other's secrets so readily? There is a pact of silence when it comes to keeping things from parents, but they sure seemed to know all about each other's private business.

| Sat
4:19pm | fu. | Dan |
| Sat
4:18pm | u r such an AH! | Dan |

Sat 4:17pm	might as well tell u cuz evry1 else knows we did it he says I suck	Dan
Sat 4:14pm	JD that fking jerk	Dan
Sat 4:06pm	boy trouble yea u could say so	Dan
Sat 4:05pm	No not chick fight	Dan
Sat 4:04pm	something happened	Dan
Sat 4:03pm	sry I'm hiding thought u wr after me 2	Dan
Sat 4:02pm	what u wanna dis me now 2?	Dan

My daughter's vulgar voice was appalling, along with her willingness to put these awful words in writing. For anyone to see. Including her mother.

Next the time stamp jumped back several hours, and I recalled that she had fallen asleep on the sofa Saturday afternoon. I had thought she was just tired. Now I could not even begin to imagine what she had been going through. I continued reading the messages she had sent.

Sat 12:43pm	I'm so tired gonna lay down awhile	Pennie
Sat 12:41pm	I thought I liked him but not now	Pennie
Sat 12:40pm	never	Pennie
Sat 12:38pm	easy for u to say hes not talking bout u	Pennie
Sat 12:37pm	finslly ur awake hes so mean telling evry1	Pennie
Sat 11:52am	get uuuuuuuuuuupppp!	Pennie
Sat 10:40am	pleeeeeeeeze call me	Pennie
Sat 9:23 am	I din sleep at all text me	Pennie

The time stamp receded back into very early Saturday morning. It broke my heart; my husband and I had been sound asleep, while our daughter was under attack.

Sat 2:56am	u told him I was bad? and evrything else?	JD
Sat 2:55am	liar	JD
Sat 2:54am	what u tell sam?	JD

Sat 2:49am	omg	Sara
Sat 2:47am	why? whats going on?	Sara
Sat 2:28 am	why would jd tell sam all that what a jerk	Pennie
Sat 2:10 am	I took a shwr when i got home	Pennie
Sat 2:09am	if u say so but its kinda gross don't u think?	Pennie
Sat 2:09am	I dunno it hurt	Pennie
Sat 2:09am	do u like it?	Pennie
Sat 2:08am	who? when?	Pennie
Sat 2:08am	?	Pennie
Sat 2:07am	tell me!	Pennie
Sat 2:07am	have u?	Pennie
Sat 2:07am	I think we rly did it	Pennie

Sat 2:06am	stop it ur a bigger slut	Pennie
Sat 2:06am	he was pushing at me and he got it in	Pennie
Sat 2:06am	I couldnt do it good so he got on top and he got my pants open	Pennie
Sat 2:05am	youve done it? I had no idea	Pennie
Sat 2:05am	sam?	Pennie
Sat 2:04am	you did that?	Pennie
Sat 2:04am	he told me suck him	Pennie
Sat 2:03am	its gross I don wanna tell u	Pennie
Sat 2:02am	we were making out and he pulled it out	Pennie
Sat 2:02am	I know	Pennie
Sat 2:01am	no they were home!	Pennie
Sat 2:01am	we were at his house in the bsmt	Pennie

Sat 2:00am	I can't believe I did it	Pennie
Sat 1:59am	I was trying to find u b4	Pennie
Sat 1:58am	but I guess he's ok to tell u	Pennie
Sat 1:58am	JD told sam already?	Pennie
Sat 1:57am	shut up! Who told u?	Pennie
Sat 1:56am	omg peewee I have news	Pennie

Of course Ali had turned to her best friend to share this special event in a young woman's life. Although the description of giving in to J. D. did not sound all that special.

It struck me that this was not something a mother should know until perhaps years later, laughing together as adult women. When that conversation occurred, could I pretend I had no previous knowledge?

The text messages continued, unfolding the entire story of what had happened between Ali and J. D., along with commentary from all of their friends.

Sat 1:55am	what time? I'll come watch	JD

Sat 1:53am	ur sweet	JD
Sat 1:52am	stop	JD
Sat 1:52am	omg no	JD
Sat 1:51am	;-)	JD
Sat 1:50am	blushing thinking about it	JD
Sat 1:49am	I didn't do it with him tho	JD
Sat 1:48am	just one	JD
Sat 1:46am	r u bigger than most guys?	JD
Sat 1:46am	im rly sore now	JD
Sat 1:45am	wait I'm talking to JD	Pennie
Sat 1:44am	was I?	JD
Sat 1:43am	could u tell I liked it?	JD

Sat 1:42am	did u like it?	JD
Sat 1:41am	bet I know 2 ha ha	JD
Sat 1:40am	wish u were here	JD
Sat 1:39am	sry ur not stupid	JD
Sat 1:37am	obviously stupid	JD
Sat 1:36am	u awake?	JD

I recalled that the other half of that late night conversation with J. D. (well, actually very early Saturday morning) had really had been quite sweet. Truncated thoughts, pecked out by fingertips, forced the communication into its most essential bits and pieces, almost like poetry. Text messaging is the new art form of this century, I thought. I continued to read Ali's "poetry".

Sat 1:34am	pleeeeeeze don't tell any1	Sam
Sat 1:33am	stop!	Sam
Sat 1:32am	omg stop it	Sam

Sat 1:31am	u can't ask that!	Sam
Sat 1:31am	mmm not sure	Sam
Sat 1:30am	first time ever	Sam
Sat 1:29am	no WITH him u kno?	Sam
Sat 1:28am	I was with JD	Sam
Sat 1:27am	u have to swear silence	Sam
Sat 1:27am	can I trust u?	Sam
Sat 1:26am	cant tell u	Sam
Sat 1:25am	she wont answer and I need to talk to her	Sam
Sat 1:24am	d u know whr she is	Sam
Sat 1:23am	is pennie with u?	Sam
Sat 1:19am	pleeeeeze call me	Pennie

Sat 1:15am	whr r u????	Pennie
Sat 1:13am	text me i have news	Pennie
Sun 3:24am	I have to move away or jump off a fucking bridge	Pennie

I had come full circle. I had gone all the way. Just like my girl.

The phone felt small and lifeless in my hand. Its enticing contents had been spilled, and now it was spent. I faced the harsh morning light with nothing but shame and regret. Like too many first times after going too far, there was no afterglow, no enfolding in warm arms, and no whispers of love. I was bound to my poor daughter by identical mistakes. We had both ventured into dangerous territory we had no business thinking we could handle, and we had both ended up embarrassed, wounded by those we thought we could trust, and achingly isolated, with only our shameful thoughts for company.

I placed the phone on the bathroom counter and went down the hall. *What now?* popped into my head like a text message that cannot be ignored. The words stayed there, stamped on the screen in my mind:

What now? What now? What now?

"No, I don't know where your socks are.
It's not my turn to find them."

OUR LUCKY DAY

*D*riving home from the hospital after working the night shift, I marveled at what a beautiful fall day it was. Across the hillsides, the sun danced off the leaves of the autumn trees radiating dazzling hues of bright yellow sunburst, jack-o-lantern orange, deep crimson, and vivid magenta under a brilliant blue sky.

My thoughts strayed to the plans for our busy day. Weekends were always a juggling act among our three sons' sports, backyard barbeques with friends, and perhaps a moment or two for each other. This particular Saturday would be filled with soccer. As luck would have it, two of the day's games were back-to-back on the same field. My husband, Drew, was the coach of our oldest son Michael's team and, in a typical handoff, the instant I stepped into the house, they were out the door heading for the team warm-up.

I quickly packed a picnic lunch for everyone and hustled our middle son, David, age seven, and our youngest, Taylor, age five, into the van along with their team equipment bags. In the rearview mirror, I could see Taylor's bowl-cut hair flying around as he incessantly taunted his brother. Taylor was a challenge—precocious, obstinate, and strong-willed. Some days I just prayed for one hour of peace.

Michael's game was exciting. As usual, he scored a goal, and his team won. After the handshake between teams, Michael and a teammate bounded over to the sidelines.

"Hey, Mom! Can Joe stay with us to watch David's game?"

Before I could even finish saying, "Sure, just let me check with Joe's mom," Michael and Joe took off in a flat-out race across the green grass, yelling, laughing, and poking at each other.

I found Joe's mom, Sue, chatting with some of the other parents.

"Here, take Joe's soccer bag," she said. "He's got a lot of allergies, and there's an epi pen in there. I'll be at home if anything comes up—here's our number."

I grabbed Michael's bag, too, and walked with Sue toward the parking lot. "Don't worry, I'm a nurse," I assured her as I tossed the bags into the back of the van. "I've dealt with plenty of emergencies." Sue waved goodbye, and I headed back to the field where David's game was starting. I spotted

Taylor running in and out of the woods behind the field with Amber, a girl he knew from school.

David's soccer game was intense. The teams were very evenly matched, and the momentum switched back and forth with tough defense on both sides. At halftime the score was 1–1.

The second half had just started when a piercing scream overwhelmed the voices of the kids on the field and the parents hollering from the sidelines. The hairs on the back of my neck stood on end, and I knew without looking that it was Taylor screaming.

Everything that happened next still seems so real, I relive it as if it is happening all over again, right now, in real time.

***

I turn in the direction of the screaming and see Taylor running out of the woods in his little black shirt with a swarm of angry bees flashing white and yellow surrounding him, *on him*. Amber is running a few steps behind, but no cloud envelops her. I run and scoop my child into my arms, and the insects loop in unison back toward the woods. Someone else's mother says, "Here, put this ice pack on his stings." Another voice rings out, "Do you have Benadryl?"

"In the van," I gasp as I struggle to run to the parking lot as fast as I can with Taylor in my arms. He is frantically shrieking and dripping sweat. His normally bouncy hair is glued to his head. Tears streak his face, but by the time I reach the car, he has stopped crying and is unusually quiet. Something is very, very wrong. He is clammy now, his arms limply hanging down instead of clasped around my neck. I fling the sliding side door open and unload him onto the seat. I grab the bottle of Benadryl from the driver's side door pocket and give him one, two, three, maybe even four teaspoons—I don't know.

He's too quiet. His lips are purple. His skin is pale. He is straining to breathe. A voice inside me is saying, "Come on, you're a trained nurse! You should know what to do!" But the nurse has not shown up; I am just a mom, an ordinary mom, helpless and panicked.

What else? *What else?* Somehow, I remember Taylor's inhaler for his occasional asthma and grab that from the console. I pump several puffs in his mouth. I cannot tell if any went in. "Taylor. Breathe in! Did any get into your lungs?" There is no response. Can he even hear me? He seems quieter and paler, and as I watch, his eyes begin to roll back, and his lids flutter closed. "No!" I scream. What else can I do? I look around, but no one has followed me to the parking lot. Where is Drew? Probably with the crowd watching the game, thinking I have the first aid completely under control.

Suddenly, my mind snaps alert. There is something else— right here in this van. I look in the back at a pile of identical, navy blue team soccer bags. Frantically, my hands shaking so badly I can barely work the zippers, I search through endless compartments on the ends, sides, and insides of the bags, finding socks, shin guards, soccer shoes, T-shirts, water bottles, gum, Band-Aids. Finally, in desperation, I dump the contents of the bags on the ground. Where is it? It's *got* to be here.

I look over at Taylor and say, "How you doing, honey?" No response again and then...*yes!* I find it in a small zippered pouch. I immediately jab Taylor's skinny little leg with the epi pen, using way too much force so his leg begins to bleed. I stand there staring at the tube in my hand, wondering if he got the medicine. The needle is exposed, but I have never used one of these before. I am just not sure.

Suddenly, another team mom is standing at my side. "How is he? What can I do?"

"Dial 9-1-1," I reply. I look over at Taylor. He is pale. His leg is bleeding. He is covered with red blotches all over his face, arms, and legs. He is quiet. But underneath his black shirt dribbled with sticky red Benadryl, his little chest is going up and down. He is breathing. And is it possible his lips do not look so purple—or is that my imagination?

Moments later, an ambulance arrives. I hear my husband directing the paramedics toward the field to go help the boy who possibly just broke his leg. "Everything is OK over here," he says, waving off the mom beside me who is trying to get their attention. But we are not OK here. Drew does not know what just happened. He does not know that Taylor had a massive allergic reaction and had been on his way to dying right here in our van.

I try to holler, "Wait!" to Drew, but no words come out of my mouth. So I just hold up the epi pen.

When the ambulance attendant sees it, he asks if I had administered it. I nod my head. He tells me that a second ambulance is on the way and that one could take care of the boy on the field. "We'll take this one first," he says to the other EMT.

They lift Taylor's thin, limp body onto the gurney and put him into the ambulance. I climb in behind. I am sure that if I turn my eyes away for even a second, he will stop breathing. We arrive at the hospital, and as Taylor is getting settled into a curtained-off examining room, I simply stand at his side and watch his little chest to be sure it is still rhythmically rising and falling.

***

When the attending physician came in, the paramedic lifted the epi pen. In a condescending tone, he told the doctor, "She gave this medicine to him, and it is prescribed to someone else. She's a nurse. She knows better. That's a no-no." In that moment, I could have strangled that man with my bare hands. I stared straight into his smug face and wanted to spit.

The doctor's voice brought me out of my venomous

stance. "Well, we should be thanking her for saving this boy's life, or at least preventing the need for a tracheotomy. She's a pretty smart nurse after all. And he's quite a lucky boy."

The examination revealed that Taylor had been stung eighteen times by white-faced hornets. The hospital sent us home with an epi pen and instructions for the entire family: Rest. "And call immediately if he has another reaction."

We drove home, where Drew was preparing supper. He had already dropped Joe off, and I remembered that I still had Joe's team bag and that he no longer had an epi pen. I called Sue to explain and apologize. "We have extras, don't worry," she said. "We've never had to use one."

Next, I called work to tell them that I would not be in and why. The remainder of the weekend was calm and quiet.

On Monday morning, it was back to business as usual. I got the two older boys ready and off to school. Then I drove Taylor to school, not really planning to leave him there. I'm not sure why. Are they familiar with epi pens and how to use them? I just wanted to keep him safe with me. And watch him breathe.

At school, I went straight to the nurse's office to explain what had happened. She listened to me very intently and then opened her medical box and showed me three epi pens, assuring me that she knew how to use them. I decided maybe it would be OK to leave Taylor at school, so I walked him to his classroom. After talking to his teacher, I headed to the office. There, the principal and secretary must have seen something on my face. "Are you OK?" they asked.

Suddenly, right in front of the entire office, I broke into uncontrollable sobbing. "He could have died. He could have died."

The trauma of that day, *my* trauma of that day, had finally sunk in. As moms do, I had kept it together for the family over the weekend. But when the reality of the situation registered, I realized that if the events of that day had not happened exactly as they had, perhaps there might have been a different, terrible outcome. What if I hadn't gone to the games and instead stayed home to get some sleep after working all night? What if Michael hadn't asked to have a friend stay with us in the park? What if Joe's mom had said "No"? And was it just serendipity that Michael asked to have a friend stay who just *happened* to have an epi pen?

Perhaps luck had played a part in the outcome. But to this day, I am also convinced that a higher power was watching over us, protecting us, and intervening on Taylor's behalf. It was not his time to go. So every day, I say a prayer of thanks that Taylor was spared. We were given an extraordinary gift on an ordinary day, a very lucky and beautiful gift.

"Where are your manners? You weren't born in a barn, you know!"

LIKE MOTHER, LIKE DAUGHTER

*I*t was a beautiful, sunny day near the end of summer vacation, and my girlfriend had just called and invited us over to swim in their pool. My daughter was four and would be starting kindergarten in the fall, so I thought this would be a fun thing for us to do before the school year started.

"Cathy, guess what? I just got off the phone with Mrs. Pile, and she wants us to come over for a swim in their pool. So, go get your bathing suit on and get together whatever toys you want to bring with you."

She went off and did as she was told. The next time I saw her, she had already donned a pink and white polka dot bikini with coordinating pink jelly shoes and was clutching a Disney *Lion King* towel and her swimmies.

I shoved my dumpy, middle-aged body into one of the many black bathing suits that was best at holding my stomach in, threw on an oversized T-shirt of my husband's, and we jumped in the car and drove the mile up the street.

Upon our arrival, we saw that Mrs. Pile was already outside with her son, Willie, her year-old daughter, and a couple of other lady friends from the neighborhood and their kids.

We all greeted each other: "Hey, Hello, Hi!" "What a great idea, a day at the pool." "We're going to have so much fun!"

The kids were running around, playing in the yard, and swimming in the pool. The moms sat talking, half-watching the kids. I scanned the yard again and realized that I had not seen Cathy in a couple of minutes. This is kind of odd, I thought. Where would she be with all the kids running around and the activities going on outside?

Quickly, I scanned the bottom of the pool to make sure that my quasi-parenting skills had not resulted in her drowning. Nope—she was not on the bottom of the pool. I then proceeded to look in the direction of the swing set. Nope—she was not there, either. I ventured around to the front of the house to see if she was out there. Nope. Well, maybe she went inside to use the bathroom.

I headed into the house and discovered that she was not in the bathroom, nor was she anywhere on the first floor. So I headed upstairs to look in the two bedrooms. Both doors were shut. I opened one; the room was empty. I opened the other door, and the sight before me made me choke on my intake of breath and the ensuing gasp of astonishment that followed.

A mom bursting into the room only slightly startled Cathy and Willie. Standing before me, in a crouched position like she was going to sit on a chair (or more likely, on Willie's face), was my rosy-cheeked daughter. And lying on the floor looking up in the direction of her hiney was her friend, Willie. Down around her ankles was the bottom of her pink and white polka dot bikini. (Mental note: No more two-piece bathing suits for her.)

I yelled in an excited and quivering voice, "What are you doing?"

My daughter responded in her innocence, "Willie's just checking things out, Mom!" as if it was no big deal.

I squelched the desire to scream at the two of them, mustered up whatever bit of calmness I could, and told Willie, "Stop looking at Cathy's fanny, and get outside and play with the other kids."

I was seething mad at my daughter, and wanted to smack the tar out of her, but I knew I could get arrested for that. Instead, I settled for planting a smack on her butt and sternly telling her, "Pull up the bottoms of your bathing suit and go outside. And you'd better behave yourself or we're going home."

She headed on her merry way while I tried to compose myself the best I could. Heading back outside to join the other moms, I kept fuming, what a *bad* girl she is. What happened to our many conversations about not showing anyone your private parts? Had she forgotten? It was only, like, yesterday! I was very angry with her for doing something she should have known was naughty and wrong.

When I reached the others, peacefully sunning themselves, I described in detail the situation I had found upstairs. Of course, they all thought it was hysterically funny (probably because it wasn't their kid) and tried to cheer me up (while laughing):

"This is the age when children start doing these types of things."

"It's normal."

"They're curious."

"Don't worry about it."

I knew they were trying to help make me feel better, but I just tuned them out. Irate thoughts kept dashing around in my head, and all I heard coming out of their mouths was "Blah, blah, blah." I sat there in my angry silence intermittently throwing dirty looks my daughter's way, only to come to the realization that she had already forgotten about what I could not seem to get off my mind.

As I sat there quietly, my mind wandered. I went back in time, to my childhood, and I suddenly heard my father's voice yelling, "What are you kids doing in there?" as he poked his head around the blanket that was our makeshift tent, posing as our hospital headquarters. Inside the tent, there were a number of kids with their pants down around their knees while the would-be doctors were taking their temperatures. And if my memory serves me correctly, that was not the only time my dad caught me in that kind of situation. I guess I was a *bad* girl, too.

As the afternoon wore on, I began to rationalize that this behavior is some sort of childhood rite of passage, entered into innocently and propelled by their complete lack of inhibitions at this age. The curiosity factor is apparently much stronger than the threat of getting in trouble for doing something that the child knows they are not supposed to do.

Just as our parents taught us right from wrong, we, in turn, have taught our children the same thing. If exploration is something that they have always done and will continue to do, despite our warnings, then we should not take these childish indiscretions as a reflection of our parenting skills.

Back at the pool, with a shrug of the shoulders, I conceded that perhaps I had overreacted. By the end of the day, I laughed to myself, and *at* myself, and decided to chalk the whole thing up to "like mother, like daughter."

"If you're going to kill each other,
do it outside!"

THE NEST

They were such fragile birds when born
Two-and-a-half pounds each, their hair looked shorn
Their little fingers and toes how I did adorn.

Each night as they nested to sleep, I hoped their dreams
soared to good places.

Two ducklings of many at day care—Bright Horizons
Grandpa called it Harvard Horizons
I called it my 'all important get back to career' horizons.

Each night as they nested to sleep, I prayed that their flight
toward their own horizons would always be bright.

We took flight when they were just two
To California to start a new life we would do
What we learned as a family flock and I now know to be true:

As we make or remake our nest, we bring along the same
feathers but also the same sticks, dirt, and worms of our lives.

The mother hen watched as her beautiful boys learned to fly
They schooled and skied under Colorado skies
They were the best of times with years of chirping sounds
— both laughs and cries.

The silence is deafening when tweet goes to full tween.

Our wings felt clipped as we lived under the vulture's hover
The sun was dimmed and the stars didn't cover
We prayed that our birds seemingly broken by drugs, alcohol,
and self-doubts would soon recover.

They did migrate into the journey of recovery; they do turn
doubt to self-definition; they fly once again.

The nest is empty and the chirps do not so cry constant
The flutter of activity does not so fly constant
The pecking at the groceries does not so fry constant.

The nest is empty, as the eagles have soared to good places,
yet they visit constant.

"A soul is healed by being with children."

English Proverb

EPILOGUE

Last summer, about fifty of our family members and friends were sharing a lighthearted sunny afternoon on the beach at Cape Cod. The little ones, slathered with sunscreen, frolicked in the ocean waves.

The men played sand bocce. Some of the women sat and read, while others wistfully noted that surely *today* all world problems would be solved. It was the kind of perfect and magical day that makes you think that way.

With eyes closed, my senses were concentrated on the sounds of the gentle rush of the ocean combined with the wonderful hum of the voices that surrounded me. Suddenly, I became aware of the deeper, louder voices of the men rising in excitement.

"Hey, what's that?"

"It's glass, watch out."

"Throw it out—the kids will get hurt on it."

"Yeah, I'll get rid of it."

"No, wait—there's something in there!"

And finally my son's voice: "Give it to me."

I opened my eyes to see Sam holding a wine bottle with a paper rolled up inside. Literally, a message in a bottle!

Talking over each other, our whole group began giving advice on how to get to the message.

"Use your finger."

"Use a stick."

"Does anyone have a knife?"

"How about a straw?"

"She has long fingers—give it to her."

I was entrusted with the bottle and the task of retrieving the message. Repeatedly, I attempted to fish out the message with my fingers, a stick, a feather, a piece of sea grass, and a corkscrew, all to no avail.

"We have been coming here for over thirty years and never found a message in a bottle," someone said.

"It is probably from somebody on vacation from across the country who wants us to send them a postcard back in reply," another said with a chuckle.

"Maybe someone is being held captive by her cruel stepfather and needs us to save her!" one of the kids imagined.

After numerous attempts and much toil, we determined that the only way to obtain our message was to break the

glass. My husband carefully smashed the lower end of the bottle against the edge of a large metal trash barrel and handed me the rolled message inside, which was accompanied by a feather and a shell. I began to read:

To the heart of my heart, my precious little girl,

It is incredible to me still that you are not with us.
I carry you in my heart. Every breath, every
thought, you are close. You are a young lady now,
15 years old, and I see you all fresh and full of
energy and life. I miss you so much. No one can
know how much. It amazes me how one can get
used to living with the shock of your loss, it is always
with me and all my happy moments are tinged with
sadness and disbelief. I long for you.
I want to touch your hair and hear you laugh. You
are my little angel. I hope you are in a beautiful and
peaceful place, and one day we will meet there and I
will know you in an instant. Until then you are in
my every thought.

I love you,
Mom

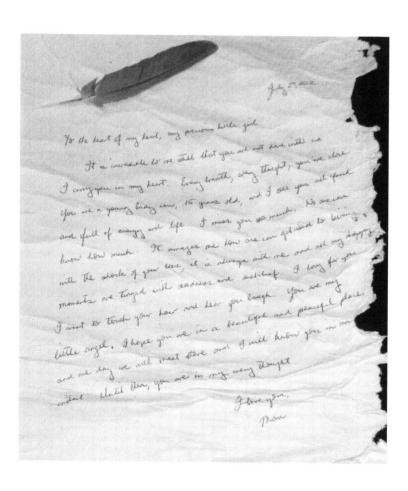

Needless to say, tears were dripping down our faces and onto the sand before I even finished reading the note. The rest of the day, our minds and our hearts stayed with the woman—the mom—who had written that beautiful message, placed it in a bottle, and launched it into the ocean. From where had the bottle been cast? How far away was the mother from us now? And how was it even possible that the bottle had come to *me*, in the middle of a book project about sharing true stories of motherhood?

***

Nary a dry eye remained at our writers' circle when I shared this story and the fragile note. We immediately knew two things: (1) This touching story had to go into the book, and (2) Wherever this mother may be, our hearts will be with her every day.

QUESTIONS FOR DISCUSSION

1. How did it make you feel to read the honest revelations of the author moms about their own child rearing experiences?

2. Which story or incident resonated with you the most? Why did that particular story touch a chord in you? What were your biggest take-aways from the stories you read?

3. In what ways is the experience of reading true stories different from reading fictional ones?

4. Why do you think the writers chose not to identify which author wrote each particular story?

5. Growing up, what was your idea of "motherhood?" As you grew up, and perhaps had children of your own, how have your views changed?

6. How have modern forces, like technology and cultural influences, changed "motherhood" over time?

7. What influence did your mom have on you as a mother?

8. "Helicopter Moms" and "Tiger Moms" are terms used currently to describe some mothers. How do you view these moms, and what would you name your own mothering style?

9.   The title of the book suggests that what we experience as mothers is somewhat common or widespread (in other words, "just ordinary"). Do you agree or disagree with this point of view? Why or why not?

10. If motherhood was genuinely recognized as extraordinary, how would that impact the world? Would there be less war, more compassion, greater tolerance, etc. or is that too idealistic?

11. How open are you with other moms when sharing your stories about your children? Does reading these stories make you feel more comfortable about revealing personal experiences?

12. Are there other stories from your life, beyond motherhood experiences, that are aching to be told?

13. What have been your best, and worst, "Mommy Moments?"

14. What do you want others to know about you as a mom?

Q&A WITH THE AUTHORS

How do eight women decide to write a book together?

Jeanne (laughing): Are you asking how do eight women agree on anything?

Bonnie: In many ways, this all started over 20 years ago, when some of us got to know each other from a Newcomers Book Club.

Linda: Remember we even had Newcomers "Mystery Dinners" and things like that?

Robin: Those were the good old days.

Caren: I still have Robin's original email dated May 25, 2009.

```
Hello Book Club Ladies,

I have a great idea! Let's write a book.
Yes I am serious…the first draft will be
due at our September 10th, 2009 book club
meeting at my house (you have the whole
summer).
```

Robin: Of course, the book project did not proceed quite as planned. Only five people showed up, and even one of those decided "no way" after discovering how serious the rest of us were!

Maureen: I got invited to join the group after Linda posted something on Facebook, asking about long-time, unfulfilled dreams, and I commented, "Someday I'd like to be a writer."

She posted back, "I think I can help you with that."

Celia: I think the fact that each of us had a professional career before we had children, and most continued to work at least part-time throughout the child rearing years and are still working today, helped us understand how to organize and finish a project as complex as this one.

Caren: And while we all had diverse backgrounds in terms of professions, circumstances, and upbringing, the one thing we all had in common was the experience of being a mother. That bonded us at the beginning and has kept us bonded all the way through.

What was it like to hear those initial stories you first presented to each other?

Celia: The first time I went to our writer's circle meeting—it was amazing! As soon as the first person began reading her story, a hush fell over the room. We roared with laughter at some moments, but also shed tears, because the emotions evoked by the stories were so powerful. Right away, we knew we had something special going on.

Maureen: We gave each other a safe setting to speak honestly about how we felt. The more we felt the trust that existed with each other, the deeper we were willing to go.

Lael: Hearing other moms speak their truths about motherhood is a form of validation, not just of the types of experiences or particular struggles, but also of the sometimes very raw emotions involved. Wonder, joy, and gratitude of course, but also more tender feelings such as anger, guilt, or helplessness. Whether or not a particular story resonated in the details, it always resonated with me emotionally, validating my own inner experience as a mother.

Why do you think it is important for women to share their stories?

Jeanne: Mothering can be very isolating. Your child might be sick or misbehaving or in trouble, sometimes other members of the family are also being impacted, and you have no idea what to do about any of it.

Maureen: In everyday conversation, we tend to put up a façade that our kids are perfect, our homes are perfect, everything is perfect, and we are in control. If we can share more heartfelt and real stories with each other, the constrictive armor of being "the perfect mother" is shed, revealing the important truth that no mother is perfect and that is OK. What a relief!

Bonnie: The experience of hearing each other's stories is also heartwarming, entertaining and encouraging. We can all use a little lightness and fun.

Lael: Also, I don't think we realized that the experience of *writing* a story would be so rewarding. Writing about fearful or painful times gave us all courage.

Caren: Every single one of us, and by that I mean mothers everywhere, has a story to tell, and each story is as important as anyone else's. It is important to know that we are all in this together. Sharing our experiences with each other empowers each person individually and women as a group.

Why did you call yourself "ordinary" moms?

(Answered collectively): We feel we are typical of many women raising a family in small town America. Middle-class, yes, although not a single one of us has been immune from life's difficulties. Divorce, job loss, financial devastation, serious illness, loss of loved ones, kids with disabilities, dysfunctional families – you name it and one of us has lived it. We hail originally from many different parts of the country and have a wide range of family backgrounds.

We also represent a variety of professions, some requiring advanced degrees and certifications: nurse, journalist, business owner, educator, psychologist, paralegal, corporate executive. Yet we have also worked as cashiers and waitresses and other more "everyday," but equally important jobs. Most of us worked through much of our child rearing years; some were single moms struggling to manage raising children alone; others were stay-at-home-moms for at least part of the time.

As for a discussion of marriages… Let's just say that is another book in itself! (Laughter from all). We are all married now, though not necessarily to the father of our children. None of us feels like we did anything extraordinary to get to where we are now; we all just did what we had to do to raise our families as best we could. Just like any other "ordinary" mom would do!

You have published these stories without attaching individual names to individual stories. Why did you decide to do that?

Linda: I remember a turning point at one writer's circle

meeting, when an author read an incredibly personal account of a situation that is not very common. Right there in that room of eight women, another author spoke up and said, in a very quiet voice, "Except for the sex of your children, that could have been *my* story." Time after time, we were floored by the universal nature of so much of what we were sharing with each other.

Lael: We also felt that our purpose—to tell stories, even painful ones, which other moms might relate to—was important. However, we recognized that other people depicted in the stories: our children, siblings, husbands, parents, and even teachers and other side "characters," may have experienced the event in a different way. We had no desire to judge, offend, or expose anyone, so we chose to change certain identifying information and to publish without identifying a story's author.

Robin: These are not just our stories—they are everyone's stories. They really do not need to have anyone's name attached to them.

Bonnie: Obviously, the privacy of anyone who might be mentioned in one of these stories is paramount, and it just made sense not to identify particular stories with individual writers in order to attempt to maintain that privacy.

You tried out some of the stories on readers groups and book clubs before you decided to move ahead and actually publish a book. What was that experience like?

Lael: Reading a few of the stories out loud to book clubs and other groups is what really convinced us to move ahead with publishing. In fact, they begged us, "Please finish the book because I just want to curl up in bed with it."

Caren: And then, when we asked whether any of them had stories to tell—oh my! Some people who seemed so quiet and reserved had the most hilarious things to say!

Celia: One of our goals is always to help others get their stories out of their heads and onto a page or into the ears of someone who will gain something from it. This has happened time after time at our readings and is incredibly fun.

What has been the reaction to the book from your children?

Jeanne: Some of them have joked that they plan to write their own book of stories about us: *Just Ordinary Kids – The Revenge!* (Laughter from all).

Maureen: Yea, we hope they won't need to go on *Dr. Phil* to get therapy after this. (More laughter).

Jeanne: Seriously, though, having felt the sting of having some of my own "less-than-stellar" mommy moments memorialized in some of my children's writings, for school assignments and such, I can appreciate that it isn't necessarily easy for our kids to read these accounts of certain challenging moments involving them. This is one of those books that, hopefully, they will read again when they have children of their own and can appreciate the adult perspective. Like my mom used to say to us when she was not happy with something one of us had done, "Just wait until you have kids of your own one day—then you'll know what it's like!" And she was right! (Laughter from all).

Robin: Many of our children (those who are old enough to understand how complex this book project was) are quite proud of us. It feels good to have your child say, "Way to go, Mom!"

Talk about the cover – it is gorgeous and humorous at the same time.

Robin: We came up with so many ideas about how the cover should look. We drew them out for each other: everything from a kitchen scene to paper dolls to a clothesline with mommy stuff hanging from it.

Caren: They were all good ideas, but we are *not* artists, believe me.

Linda: We had heard about online graphic design contests and decided to hold one. Within days, we had dozens of designers presenting over a hundred ideas that we had never even thought of. We were so excited!

Maureen: The cover we ultimately selected represents so much about motherhood: Mom and apple pie, primary colors, balancing home and work, multi-tasking, humor, and elegance. This design just grabbed our attention. It's perfect.

Who inspires you?

"Anyone who overcomes adversity to live her dream."

"All of the strong women in my family who gave me roots and wings."

"My grandmother, one of the original turn-of-the-century Women's Libbers."

"Women who are trying to change the world."

"My child for the way she has learned to navigate her world."

"My fellow authors from this book."

"Writers everywhere."

"My mother, of course!"

Who are some of your favorite authors?

(Answered collectively): Pearl Buck, Dale Carnegie, Ken Follett, Deborah Harkness, Stephen King, Wally Lamb, Anne Lamott, Gregory Maguire, Yann Martel, James Patterson, Dave Pelzer, Norman Vincent Peale, Jodi Picoult, Anna Quindlen, Anne Rivers Siddons, Irving Stone, Anne Tyler, Abraham Verghese, Tom Wolfe.

Why did you choose to donate a portion of the book proceeds to charities for women and children?

Celia: Most of us are volunteers for charitable purposes in some form or fashion. Several are on not-for-profit boards, others serve on community commissions, some are heavily involved in church activities— everyone has a cause or causes they support already.

Bonnie: As a group, we feel that we would like to make a difference in the future lives of women and children, both through the power of story and the power of charity. We liked the idea of donating locally, nationally, and globally.

What's next on the horizon for the group?

Jeanne: Our calendars are filling up with reading events, TV and radio appearances, library gatherings, fundraisers; we had no idea we would be so busy this quickly.

Linda: And, we are already collecting stories for future books. *Just Ordinary Moms* seems to have struck a chord, providing inspiration and courage to "ordinary" people and encouraging them to share their most heartfelt stories so that others may benefit. We look forward to publishing these wide-ranging stories from "just ordinary" folks for years to come.

Do you have any advice or words of wisdom for other "just ordinary" moms?

"Enjoy the ride!"

"Keep a journal. Every day or every week, write down a paragraph about each of your children, capturing those little moments that are fleeting, but mean so much."

"Be kind to yourself."

"Work less, mom more."

"Be empathetic: to other mothers, your children, and yourself."

"As bad as you think things are at the moment, it will pass. Life will go on and everybody will get through it."

"Share yourself with your kids, your family, and your friends. And especially with other moms!"

"When you lay your head down at night, give thanks for your kids and ask for strength and courage for the next day."

Any closing thoughts?

Robin: None of us holds a degree in child counseling. We are not physicians or specialists in child rearing in any way. We are just moms, ordinary moms, who love our children and have tried to do our very best. Are our children perfect? No. And if your best friend attempts to tell you how perfect her children are she obviously has blinders on 24/7. All of the children in this book have turned into amazing individuals. We are so blessed to be part of their world. They have survived and so have we (although we all had our doubts at times.) When you have that terrible experience with your child (we say *when* because it *will* happen because they are human and so are you), please do not beat yourself up with guilt. You are not alone and never will be again. All of us moms are in this together!

JUST FOR FUN ~ THE PB&J MARTINI

2 ounces Frangelico
1/2 ounce crème de cassis
1 ounce vodka
scant 1/2 cup Concord Grape and Black
Cherry 100% Juice
(or 100% Concord Grape juice)

Cherry or red grape for garnish

Directions:
Place all ingredients into a shaker filled
with ice. Shake for 15 seconds and then
strain into a martini glass.

Garnish with
cherry or red grape.

Serve and enjoy!

TELL US YOUR STORY

Are you a mom, dad, grandparent or kid with a story to tell? We want to hear from you! We are seeking stories for upcoming books. You could become a published author, earn royalties, and have tons of fun, all while helping others.

We are particularly interested in hearing from "Military Moms." As America winds down operations in Afghanistan and Iraq, and your children come home, we recognize that your stories will be vital to individuals, families and a nation trying to heal.

Don't worry if you are not a "writer"—you can work on crafting and polishing your narrative over time. It is the universal truth of your story we are interested in, first and foremost.

Please use the included bonus section entitled "My Story" Workshop to guide you. Then please go online and tell us about your story at www.JustOrdinaryMoms.com.

"There is nothing to writing. All you do is sit down at a typewriter and bleed."

Ernest Hemingway

BONUS SECTION:

"MY STORY" WORKSHOP

WORKSHOP INSTRUCTIONS

This workshop is intended to be a thought-provoking and helpful guide to writing the kind of story that could be published in a future Just Ordinary™ book.

The workshop consists of exercises and activities to:
- Stimulate ideas
- Discover personal truths
- Develop story "themes"
- Engage the reader
- Encourage creative and interesting use of language
- Include dialogue to add life and realism
- Incorporate all five senses into descriptions
- Layer and enrich your stories.

The workshop is not intended to be a substitute or replacement for educational writing classes, professional assistance such as editing and other services, or reader critique and review.

STIMULATE IDEAS

Each of the stories in Just Ordinary Moms contains events, conversations, descriptions, and ideas that evoke emotion, which is the best way to engage with readers.

Exercise: Examine each of the JOM stories/poems and identify at least one thing from each that invokes emotion. Capture your answers here.

The Beach Chair	
The Good Mother	
Mental Brakes	
Mother's Day	
Tempest on a Teacup	
The Ski Trip (Poem)	
Tell It Like It Is—Trilogy	
Labor Days	
Growing Tech	
Just an Ordinary Day	
My Legacy of Choice	
Million-Dollar Mom	
Click	
Caught Unaware	
Losing My Virginity	
Our Lucky Day	
Like Mother, Like Daughter	
The Nest (Poem)	
Epilogue	

STIMULATE IDEAS (continued)

Exercise: Using the emotions you found within the JOM stories, think of an event in your life that evoked a similar emotion.

Capture your answers here.

Emotion	Event

CREATE CONNECTION

Exercise: Consider each of your potential story events from the previous page. Answer these questions about any or all of them:

1. Why did this event have such an impact on me?
2. In what ways is this event universal—that is, might have a similar impact on a reader?
3. In what ways can my experience help another?

_____

_____

_____

_____

_____

_____

_____

_____

_____

_____

_____

_____

_____

_____

DEVELOP THEMES

Exercise: Consider your answers about Creating Connection. Do you notice any common themes running through? Weaving themes through a story helps it "hang together" for a reader, connecting the beginning, middle, and end.

Themes noticed:

_____

_____

_____

_____

_____

_____

_____

Additional themes I feel might be important to include in one or more of my stories:

_____

_____

_____

_____

_____

_____

STORY STRUCTURE

The opening paragraph must grab the reader, get them hooked and wanting to read more. The middle must be more than just a narration of what happened. How will you make the story interesting? The end must either wrap the story up all nice and tidy "in a bow," or leave the reader with something to think about—some reason the story is not ended tidily.

Exercise: Write five possible opening sentences to one or more of your possible stories.

_____

_____

_____

_____

_____

_____

_____

Exercise: What else will your opening paragraph include? Setting? Character introduction? Background information? Premonition of events to come? Hints at theme(s)?

_____

_____

_____

_____

WRITE IT!

Write out your story on a separate document, either by hand or on your computer. Keep working it and reworking it, using the material you have gathered here. Try not to worry about perfection at this point, simply let your words flow.

Helpful hints for getting your story out of your head and onto paper:

CHOOSE a time each day you are going to sit down and write for at least 15 minutes.

CREATE a place that feels right for writing – quiet with no distractions, comfortable, well lit, and conducive to being creative.

IF GETTING STARTED is difficult, begin by writing the ending first. This will give you a finishing point to aim for. Be prepared, however, to find that your writing takes you in a different direction, and be willing to consider alternative endings.

PICTURE the story in your mind as if you are watching a movie to capture the tiny details that will make your story come alive.

INSTEAD of writing, try speaking your story into a recording device, or record yourself telling your story to someone else. Transcribe it from the recording.

REVISIONS

The purpose of revisions is to make changes to your story, not just correct the spelling and grammar (that is editing.) Revisions often involve substantial changes. Take a step back from your story and honestly assess where major revisions could improve the flow, the plot, the characterizations, etc.

Exercises:

FLOW and STRUCTURE – Rethink the order of how you reveal the events. Sometimes starting a little ahead and looking back is effective; sometimes jumping ahead can work.

PACING - Rewrite sentences so that some are short are some are long. Short sentences are useful to create tension and describe action. Longer prose can relax the reader.

ALTERNATIVES – Use analogies, alliteration, repetition, contrasts, lyricism, and other techniques to make your writing more interesting.

DIALOGUE – Replace narrative wherever possible with dialogue to move the plot along.

CHARACTERS – Develop a full profile of each important character in the story so that they come to life for the reader.

MOOD – Create the scene: lighting, temperature, visuals, sounds, smells, etc.

EDITING - Look up *all* questions you have about using proper grammar and punctuation. Double check spelling!

ADD DETAILS

Details and descriptions help to paint a picture for the reader, bringing your story to life. Go through your story and find places to add details. Try to include descriptions that stimulate all five senses.

Exercises:

Write five different descriptions of brown hair.

_____

_____

Describe five different sounds heard at a grocery store.

_____

_____

Describe five smells in a house.

_____

_____

Describe five textures you can see right now.

_____

_____

Describe five tastes which are acrid, sweet, salty, bland and spicy without using those words.

_____

_____

_____

READER REVIEW

Writing your personal stories can serve many purposes. Some stories you may wish to simply keep within your personal diary. However, if you intend to attempt to have a story published, there is nothing more useful than asking others to read it and give you feedback.

Exercise: Choose five people with varied backgrounds who you will ask to read your story. Afterwards, request honest feedback. Make sure to thank them for their time.

Who will I ask?

_____

_____

_____

_____

Feedback given:

_____

_____

_____

_____

Now, go back and revise, revise, and revise some more. Repeat until your story is "done." Congratulations!

Made in the USA
Charleston, SC
21 April 2013